EDITOR: MARTIN WINDROW

OSPREY MILITARY · **ELITE SERIES** · 49

THE GURKHAS

Text and colour plates by
MIKE CHAPPELL

First published in Great Britain in 1994 by
Osprey Publishing, Elms Court, Chapel Way,
Botley, Oxford OX2 9LP, United Kingdom.

© Copyright 1994 Osprey Publishing Ltd.
Reprinted 1995 (twice), 1996, 1998

ISBN 1 85532 3575

Filmset in Great Britain
Printed through World Print Ltd, Hong Kong

FOR A CATALOGUE OF ALL BOOKS PUBLISHED BY OSPREY
MILITARY, AUTOMOTIVE AND AVIATION PLEASE WRITE TO:

The Marketing Manager, Osprey Publishing, PO Box 140,
Wellingborough, Northants, NN8 4ZA, United Kingdom

or visit Osprey's website at:
http://www.osprey-publishing.co.uk

Acknowledgements
The author would like to thank two serving officers for
their help in the preparation of this book: Major Ted
Shields of the 10th Princess Mary's Own Gurkha
Rifles, and Major Patrick Gouldsbury of the 6th
Queen Elizabeth's Own Gurkha Rifles. Their
generosity in the provision of photographs is much
appreciated.

Artist's Note
Readers may care to note that the original paintings
from which the colour plates in this book were
prepared are available for private sale. All
reproduction copyright whatsoever is retained by the
Publishers. All enquiries should be addressed to:

Mike Chappell
14 Downlands
Walmer
Deal
Kent CT14 7XA

The Publishers regret that they can enter into no
correspondence upon this matter.

THE GURKHAS

INTRODUCTION

Over the centuries the trade of the mercenary soldier has flourished as men with martial inclinations, the warrior races, have continued to seek service in the pay of foreign powers. Examples are many and, in Europe, have included the Swiss, the Scots and the Irish. The present troubled century has seen the employment of mercenaries in many of its wars, ranging from the sordid activities of small groups of white mercenaries in Africa to the more creditable record of the long-established French Foreign Legion.

Great Britain has had a long-standing tradition of engaging foreigners to fight in her wars, especially in the late 18th and early 19th centuries when, amongst others, large numbers of Germans were recruited to fight under the British flag in America, and on the Continent against Napoleon.

Capturing the spirit of 'the happy warrior' perfectly, a Gurkha Rifleman of 43 Indian Infantry Brigade tests the edge of his kukri; Italy, 1944. 43 Brigade consisted of three Gurkha battalions in what was called a 'lorried infantry' role. The brigade was attached to the British 1st Armoured Division at the time, and our subject wears the sign of that division. (Major H. E. Sheilds)

The last remaining vestige of this tradition is Britain's present-day Brigade of Gurkhas, a group of regiments with nearly two centuries of continuous service to a foreign monarch. Over this period the British Army's and public's respect, admiration and affection for the Gurkha soldier have grown to such a level that few would challenge the right of the Gurkha regiments to be considered an elite—and a popular elite at that. This is all the more creditable when compared with the public image of other elites, and particularly mercenary elites. A few have been loathed, many have been feared, some have been respected; but no other group of mercenaries approaches the popularity of the Gurkhas.

Gurkhas take their name from the small principality of Gorkha, which by the middle of the 18th century had conquered most of what is today known as Nepal. The King of Gorkha and his successors became so powerful that they overran the whole of the hill country from the border of Kashmir to the east of Bhutan. Turning south, they began to raid into the territories of Britain's Honourable East India Company. This was a situation that could not be tolerated by 'John Company', which declared war against the Gurkhas in 1814. There followed a series of bloody campaigns until a peace treaty was signed in the spring of 1816. The treaty gave the East India Company the right to raise battalions of Gurkhas for service in the Bengal Presidency; and since that time the rulers of Nepal have allowed their subjects to serve in the armies of certain foreign powers. These mercenaries continue to be known as Gurkhas—although there is no consensus as to who, among the Nepalese, is or is not a Gurkha.

In the years since the first Gurkha regiments were formed these Nepalese hillmen, small of stature but possessing most of the qualities that make ideal infantrymen, have gained a fearsome reputation in war. Like all reputations, this needs to be closely studied if it is to be understood and fully appreciated. Much of it is based solidly on the documented history of the Gurkha regiments and their achievements in battle. Some of it is apocryphal—and some of this, unworthy. In their time the Gurkhas, like all fighting men, have had not only their triumphs but also their setbacks; history proves them to be first-class soldiers, but not invincibles. And yet the legendary aura

Rifleman of the 3rd Gurkhas, c.1886. The uniform was rifle green with black buttons, cap and equipment; the latter was similar to the British valise equipment. The weapon is the .577 inch Snider single-shot breech-loading rifle; introduced into service with the Indian Army in the middle 1870s, it was in use until the late 1880s.

that surrounds the Gurkha fighting man continues to grow. Why this should be so is difficult to explain, but may be in part by two observed characteristics that have been common to all Gurkha soldiers since they came out of the hills to take foreign service.

The first might be described by the appellation awarded to them by so many, 'the happy warriors'. Gurkhas are cheerful men, proud and content to be soldiers, and capable of finding humour in the direst of circumstances. This attitude is the opposite of that of most Westerners, who enjoy neither soldiering nor the risks of battle, but admire those who appear to do so. The second is the mystery that continues to surround them when so few foreigners are able to speak their language, visit their homeland, or understand the complexities of their customs and religion. Those who have served alongside them have usually been delighted, if at times baffled by the experience, while developing a great respect for them. That the British officers in command of Gurkha troops have got to know and understand them better than any others goes without saying, and it is mainly through their efforts that much of the Gurkhas' history has been set down.

The story of the Gurkha regiments has been told many times, and holds a special fascination for writers and artists alike. Beyond the world of books, the 'folklore' of the Gurkhas—the stories passed on by word of mouth by generations of British soldiers, and certainly embellished in the retelling—has created quite another image in the public imagination, one that is perhaps undeserved and sometimes unintentionally demeaning. What needs to be understood is that the history and the anecdotes have been told by others—never the Gurkhas themselves. Until fairly recently the Gurkha soldier suffered from either a lack of education or from a poor one, and was therefore unable to publish his own story. With improvements in education perhaps the day is not far off when the world will be treated to the Gurkha story

in a voice from the ranks. Until this happens the story of these sterling and fascinating soldiers must continue to be told by others.

The present is a particularly poignant time to retell the story of the Gurkha regiments. Great

The rear view of the uniform worn in the previous photograph is well shown in this painting by Lieutenant A. C. Lovett, Gloucestershire Regiment, a prolific—and perhaps the best—painter of Indian Army subjects. Here his subject is Rifleman Chandra Singh Gurung of the 4th Gurkhas. Note the waterbottle, haversack, extra ammunition pouch and folded blanket strapped to the braces. The kukri is well illustrated, and balances the bayonet for the Snider worn on the left hip.

A group of 2nd Gurkhas, 1890s, in field service khaki: left to right, a bugler and a subedar in drill order, three signallers manning visual signalling equipment, and two riflemen in marching order. The piled rifles are the .45 inch Martini-Henry introduced in the late 1880s, and the equipment is similar to the British 1882 valise pattern. Note the black puttees, the heliograph mirrors on the tripod, and the signalling flags.

Britain, the principal employer of the Gurkha soldier from 1815 to 1947 and the secondary employer since the partition of India, is cutting her armed forces following the ending of the so-called Cold War. Hong Kong, the base of what remains of Britain's Brigade of Gurkhas, is to be handed back to the Republic of China before the end of the century. In the light of these events the future for Britain's Gurkha regiments looks grim. Even if a way is found to continue their service to the British Crown, it will almost certainly be in very small numbers, leading to the disappearance through amalgamation of some of the most famous of the old regiments. Against this sad prospect it should be remembered that India continues to employ a very large Brigade of Gurkhas, comprising seven regiments organised into 46 battalions—a force much larger than the British Indian Army Gurkhas before the Second World War, or Britain's Brigade of Gurkhas since 1947. The future of the Gurkha mercenary would seem, therefore, to be more secure than ever, even though they may one day no longer be able to take the pay of the British. The demand for Gurkha troops has grown steadily since the early 19th century; there is every reason to believe that the 21st century may see them employed more extensively than ever before.

The Gurkha and his homeland

Nepal is a country of some 5,500 square miles which lies along the southern slopes of the Himalayas: a narrow tract of land about 500 miles long and 100 miles wide. To the north lies Tibet, and to the south India. The topography of the Kingdom of Nepal is complex, mainly consisting of hills, forests and mountain slopes which even today enjoy only primitive communications. Large rivers drain the snows of the mountains and deeply scar the land. Life is hard

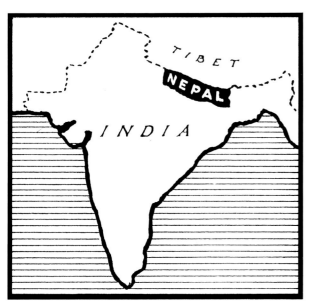

and meagre for those Nepalese who struggle to cultivate crops on the terraced hillsides or herd their flocks on the mountain slopes. It is no wonder that these farmers and shepherds have developed into a

Drummer and pipers of the 5th Gurkhas, 1890s. Many, but not all, of the Gurkha regiments have adopted the Scottish custom of pipe and drum music. Tartans have varied from the family setts of commanding officers, through those *'borrowed' from Scottish regiments to plain rifle green. The custom of pipe music is one sign of the close relationship between Gurkha and Scottish regiments that has developed over the years. See also Plate C4.*

tough and resilient stock who have brought these qualities to their soldiering for generations.

It is mainly from the yeoman stock of the cultivators and herdsmen of Nepal that recruits for military service have been chosen, the recruiting agencies confining themselves to certain tribes and clans considered to be 'martial' while avoiding (except in times of war) the tribes thought to be less suitable for the Gurkha regiments. Those considered to be the 'true Gurkha martial tribes' are the Thakur, Chhetri, Gurung, Magar, Rai, Limbu, Sunwar and Tamang, but other tribes have been enlisted from time to time.

With the exception of the tribes with a mix of

Rajput blood (such as the Chhetri, who are darker, taller, and have more Aryan features) the Gurkha soldier is Mongolian in appearance, thickset, fair-skinned, and of an average height of 5 feet 3 inches. Accustomed in civil life to carrying heavy loads in mountainous country, he has well-developed leg muscles.

The Gurkha brings to soldiering a developed character that is normally cheerful, with a keen sense of humour. Self-confident and independent, he has a fondness for strong drink—especially British Army rum—and an even greater fondness for gambling. The Gurkha is also recorded as being fond of the ladies; his religion permits polygamy, although he rarely takes more than two wives. By nature truthful and honest, he takes naturally to soldiering, considering it a calling that is both manly and desirable.

Gurkhas are Hindu, but there is a mix of Buddhism and animism in their religion that varies from tribe to tribe and among clans. However, the people of Nepal are tolerant of the beliefs of others and have never fought a religious war. Each Nepalese tribe has its own language, but the lingua franca of the country is Nepali, called Gurkhali by the British Army. Up until the late 1930s most recruits spoke only their own dialects, but today most speak Gurkhali.

The diet of a Gurkha carries certain religious restrictions, as well as those of tribe and custom. In the British Army, however, Gurkhas serving overseas are excused from all caste restrictions as to food except that they may not eat beef in any form. Before proceeding home Gurkhas undergo a purification ceremony, after which a return is made to dietary restrictions.

The Gurkha is a long-service soldier, keen to serve and to join his kinsmen in a battalion of long-service men. Careful selection at the Gurkha induction centres ensures that only the fittest and the best are chosen from the many hopefuls who apply. The system is, quite simply, beyond fault. From a reservoir of volunteers, a careful selection feeds a supply of manpower into the training centre and thence to the battalions, where experienced long-service officers and NCOs bring them on to a high standard of training and efficiency. Time is not necessarily of the essence, and in such a situation standards of efficiency are possible quite beyond those of short-service or conscript armies.

When the strain of casualty replacement or the

MESSENGER
THE OSPREY MILITARY PUBLISHING JOURNAL

OSPREY
PUBLISHING

The MESSENGER is the official journal of Osprey Military Publishing. Published 4 times a year, it includes a wide range of in-depth articles, reviews and information about forthcoming Osprey Military and Aviation books. To receive a free copy and details of how to subscribe, please fill in your name and address details below.

Please tell us your primary area of interest (please tick):

1 HISTORY

2 MODELLING

3 WARGAMING

4 OTHER

Internet Subscriber (yes/no): _____

Please tell us the title of the book in which you found this card

_____

Name: (Block letters please) Title: _____ Initial: _____

Surname: _____

Address: _____

_____

Postcode: _____ **Tel:** _____

Please affix stamp if posted from outside UK

Osprey Direct
Freepost MID16397
Wellingborough
Northants
NN8 4BR
England

aising of wartime battalions occurs, the Gurkha ystem can become diluted and less efficient. This ituation occurred in both World Wars, when re-ruiting was extended to tribes other than those martial' clans already mentioned, and when time available for training was limited. The increasing omplexity of the infantryman's trade over the years f the 20th century has called for men of greater ducation and technical ability. The operation of nechanical transport, radio communications and upport weapons in particular demands men of ptitude and requires much training time—ommodities not readily available in wartime. And et there is no evidence to show that the Gurkha egiments failed to cope with the expansions, the asualties, the curtailing of training time or the new nd complex weapons and equipment of both World Vars, and the Second World War especially.

Nor have the Gurkha regiments of the Indian Army suffered in efficiency as a result of losing the nfluence of British officers since Independence. It vas felt that the leadership of British officers was a ital and necessary ingredient to the Gurkha regi-nents up to 1947, and that their replacement by ndian officers would cause a loss of efficiency,

perhaps of fighting spirit amongst the Gurkhas. Time has proved this not to be so, much to the credit of the Gurkha soldiers of the Indian Army and their leaders.

His service over, the Gurkha soldier has been content to return to his homeland and his former way of life, no doubt made somewhat easier by the military pension paid to him. In the past at least some Gurkhas took their discharge in India, Assam or Burma, creating Gurkha communities in these places rather than returning to the hard life of the Nepalese hills. But in the main the Gurkha seems to have been unimpressed by his contact with the world outside Nepal, returning to his family, community and work with little fuss or complaint.

THE REGIMENTS

The circumstances that brought Gurkha troops into the service of the British have already been men-tioned. They were originally used by the Honourable East India Company to 'keep the peace', and saw action in a series of campaigns that included the Pindaree and Sikh Wars in 1817 and 1846. The first battle honour awarded to the Gurkha battalions was Bhurtpore in 1825. In the Indian Mutiny of 1857 the Gurkhas demonstrated their loyalty and steadfast-ness in a manner beyond praise. Active service followed in Burma, Afghanistan, the North-East and North-West Frontiers of India, Somaliland, Malta, Cyprus, Malaya, South Africa and China.

A shooting team of the 10th Gurkhas, 1905, in a photograph illustrating the khaki drill of the early 1900s. Note the slouch hats, recently adopted, and the method of wearing them. Note also the shorts, another innovation. Rifles are the .303 inch Lee-Enfield which had by now replaced the Martini-Henry. Pouches and belts are those from the equipment set shown in the previous photograph. The officers wear the standard jackets of the time, and these differ considerably from the shirt-like garment worn by the Gurkha personnel. Note the cartridge loops on the left breasts and the whistles worn by the NCOs. (Major H. E. Shields)

Before 1886 only five regiments had the title 'Gurkha'. From that year the Gurkha regiments were expanded and recruiting was put on a proper footing, with Gurkhas enlisted into the newly formed regi-ments and into the military police battalions of Assam and Burma. By this time the Gurkha soldier had proved his worth in war, and his services were much sought after. Ten regiments were eventually formed into the Indian 'line', each regiment comprising two battalions. In the Great War 200,000 Gurkhas answered the call to arms, serving in France and Flanders, Mesopotamia, Persia, Egypt and the Suez Canal zone. Gallipoli, Salonika and Palestine. An eleventh regiment was formed, and extra battalions to each regiment were raised. Between the World Wars the Gurkhas fought in the Third Afghan War and in

the campaigns on the North-West Frontier, particularly in Waziristan.

In the Second World War there were no fewer than 40 Gurkha battalions, in addition to eight of the Nepalese Army, and parachute, training, garrison and porter units: in all, nearly a quarter of a million men. The Gurkhas fought in Syria, the Western Desert, Italy, Greece, Malaya, Singapore and Burma. Casualties suffered by Gurkha units in the two World Wars exceeded 43,000.

From 1945 until the partition of India Gurkha units again 'kept the peace' in Palestine, the Dutch East Indies, Indochina and Borneo, and during the bloody division of British India between India and Pakistan in 1947, when the old Indian Army divided to serve the two newly independent states. At the time of partition there were ten Gurkha regiments and, as a result of negotiations between the Nepalese, Indian and British governments, four regiments were transferred to the British Army while the remainder stayed in the service of India. India subsequently raised the 11th Gurkhas once more, and several additional battalions of each of her regiments.

When the units of the British Brigade of Gurkhas moved to the Far East in 1948, they, with other units of the British Army already there, were formed into a division allotted the number 17 which, being largely Gurkha, was designated the 17th Gurkha Infantry Division. The original 17th Indian Division had been formed at the beginning of the Second World War, and took the 'Black Cat' as the divisional sign; it fought through the Burma Campaign from beginning to end. Its composition had been largely Gurkha, and it consisted of 48, 63 and 99 Brigades. The Brigades of the new 17th Gurkha Infantry Division were designated 48, 63 and 99 Gurkha Infantry Brigades; the Black Cat divisional sign was retained, together with crossed kukris, the sign carried by the Gurkha

Havildar of the 5th Gurkhas, 1919. W. Luker painted this NCO as one of the Indian Army contingent to a victory parade in England. His painting illustrates well the uniform worn by Gurkhas in the Middle East during the Great War. Note the double rifle-green fold in the puggaree and the shoulder title '5G'. Belt and pouches are from the 1903 pattern Bandolier equipment, and the rifle is the .303 inch Short Lee-Enfield Mk III. The badge of rank is unusual; the wearer may be a Staff Havildar Instructor of Musketry, or a havildar wearing a 'best shot' badge above his stripes. See also Plate E2.

43 Brigade in Italy. The Brigade of Gurkhas, the 17th Gurkha Division and its Infantry Brigades therefore had their origins some in the distant, some in the recent past; but each name and each number had a meaning and a tradition behind it. After 1948 additional units were raised to join the eight battalions of the Brigade of Gurkhas, namely the Gurkha Independent Parachute Company, 5 Gurkha Dog Company, the Gurkha Engineers, the Gurkha Signals, and the Gurkha Transport Regiment.

During the post-Second World War period the Brigade of Gurkhas operated continuously for twelve years against Communist terrorists throughout the Malayan 'emergency', and the Gurkha soldier once again proved himself a superb jungle fighter. A peaceful period of two years which then followed proved invaluable, as it enabled units to widen their professional horizons and train for roles other than operating against terrorists in the Malayan jungle. This was a period of intensive training which embraced all aspects of warfare likely to be encountered in South-East Asia.

The 1st/2nd Gurkhas were the first to be used again in an operational role, in Brunei during the revolt in December 1962. There followed four years of continuous operations against units of the Indonesian Army in Borneo and Sarawak in which all units of the Brigade of Gurkhas took part. It was in November 1965 that Lance-Corporal Rambahadur Limbu of the 2nd Battalion, 10th Princess Mary's Own Gurkha Rifles won the Victoria Cross, the first to be awarded in the British Army since the Korean War and the thirteenth to be won by a Gurkha soldier. With the end of the Borneo campaign in 1966 a short lull occurred before the Brigade found itself engaged in the task of 'keeping the peace' in Hong Kong, Kowloon and on the border between China and the New Territories of Hong Kong.

From 1966 Britain began another reduction of armed forces which struck at the Brigade of Gurkhas, reducing it from its peak strength of 14,000 to less than half that figure in five years. Of late, the British Gurkhas have consisted of three battalions with Gurkha signals, engineers and transport units in Hong Kong, one battalion in Brunei, and one in the United Kingdom. In 1982 the UK battalion was the 7th Gurkhas who, as part of the British task force, fought to expel the Argentines from the Falkland Islands.

The Gurkha regiments with the Indian Army went from strength to strength with five, six and in

Lieutenant-Colonel C. G. Borrowman of the 4th Gurkhas was a fine artist who drew from life and made many spirited studies. Here he has captured a bugler of the 2nd/4th Gurkhas in 1929 sounding a call. The subject wears fighting order equipment of the '08 pattern, flannel 'greyback' shirt, shorts, hosetops and short puttees. At the time the 2nd/4th wore a black leather band around the Gurkha hat instead of a puggaree. The practice of covering the scabbard of the kukri—and sometimes the bayonet—with khaki cloth appears to stem from about this time.

one case seven battalions to each of the seven regiments. In 1950 India became a republic, causing the titles of many regiments to be reviewed as royal patronage was shed. India's Gurkhas had become 'Ghorkhas', in the interest of linguistic purity, in 1949. Like their British Army counterparts the Indian Army Gurkhas have seen their fair share of active service in the turmoil of the sub-continent; and as India continues to be a strong supporter of the United Nations, her Gurkhas have served with many of the UN peace-keeping contingents.

Gurkhas also serve in the Nepalese Army and, in the past, have served in non-Gurkha regiments of the Indian Army; but these fall outside the scope of this book, which deals with the lineage, service, honours, insignia and dress distinctions of the regiments in British and Indian service.

(Over the years the spelling of the name Gurkha has had many forms, including Goorkha and Gorkha. In order to avoid unnecessary complication the current British interpretation, Gurkha, has been used throughout this narrative except when referring to changes of title. The abbreviated forms of title—e.g. 8th Gurkhas, 2nd/10th Gurkhas, etc.—used throughout imply no disrespect but are used in the interest of simplification and brevity.)

THE 1st GORKHA RIFLES (THE MALAUN REGIMENT)

The current headdress badge of the Regiment is shown at top centre. Prior to 1950 the Regiment wore the badge at bottom centre, as the 1st King George V's Own Gurkha Rifles (The Malaun Regiment). The numeral at left was worn on headdress in the late 19th century. At right is the Regiment's shoulder title from the early 1900s.

The 1st Gurkhas were raised from captured enemy troops during the Nepal War in 1815, and were known initially as the 1st and 2nd Nasiri (friendly) Battalions, the 2nd being reduced after 15 years of existence. The 1st Nasiri won its first battle honour at Bhurtpore in 1826, and fought at Aliwal and Sobraon in the first Sikh War. Following the mutiny and disbandment of the 66th Bengal Native Infantry in 1849 the Nasiri assumed the title, colours and arms of the disgraced regiment to become, in 1850, the 66th or Goorkha Regiment, Bengal Native Infantry.

In 1861 the 66th were renumbered as the 11th

BNI, but before the year was out were redesignated as the first regiment of the new Gurkha Line, becoming the 1st Goorkha Regiment (Light Infantry), while retaining the red coats they had inherited in 1849. In this distinction the 1st were unique among the Gurkha regiments, rejoicing in the description of the Lal Kurti Paltan (red-coat regiment). When a second battalion was raised in 1886 it was dressed in the rifle-green of the other Gurkha regiments, and two years later the 1st Battalion reluctantly conformed.

Subsequent changes of title for the Regiment were: 1891, 1st Gurkha (Rifle) Regiment; 1901, 1st Gurkha Rifles; 1903, 1st Gurkha Rifles (The Malaun Regiment); 1906, 1st Prince of Wales's Own Gurkha Rifles (The Malaun Regiment); 1910, King George's Own Gurkha Rifles (The Malaun Regiment).

During the Great War the 1st Battalion served in France, Mesopotamia and Egypt, while the 2nd Battalion remained on duty in India. A 3rd Battalion was raised in 1917, remaining in India until disbanded in 1921. In 1937 the Regiment underwent yet another change of title, becoming the 1st King George V's Own Gurkha Rifles (The Malaun Regiment).

Five battalions of the Regiment saw service during the Second World War. The 1st Battalion served in Egypt, Burma and Indochina, the 2nd Battalion in Malaya, where they went into Japanese

captivity on the capitulation of Singapore (being reconstituted in 1946 by the redesignation of the 3rd Battalion). The 3rd Battalion was raised in 1940 and served in Burma and Indochina. A 4th Battalion came into existence in 1941 and served in Burma and Siam before being disbanded in 1946. The 5th Battalion existed in India from 1942 to 1946.

In 1947 the 1st Gurkhas was one of the regiments selected to serve India. From 1950 they ceased to be 'King George V's Own', adopting the present title of the 1st Gorkha Rifles (The Malaun Regiment). Since 1947 new 3rd, 4th and 5th Battalions have been raised; and the 1st Gorkhas have seen a full measure of action in the service of India—as may be seen by the battle honours awarded to the Regiment since that time.

The full list of the Regiment's honours includes: Bhurtpore, Aliwal, Sobraon, Afghanistan 1878–80, Tirah, Punjab Frontier, Givenchy 1914, Neuve Chapelle, Ypres 1915, St Julien, Festubert 1915, Loos, France and Flanders 1914–15, Megiddo, Sharon, Palestine 1918, Tigris 1916, Kut-al-Amara 1917, Baghdad, Mesopotamia 1916–18, North-West Frontier India 1915–17, Afghanistan 1919, Jitra, Kampar, Malaya 1941–42, Shenam Pass, Bishenpur, Ukhrul, Myinmu Bridgehead, Kyankse 1945, Burma 1942–45, Jammu and Kashmir 1965, Darsana, Jammu and Kashmir 1971, East Pakistan 1971.

The main dress distinction of the 1st Gorkhas were the scarlet facings adopted after the regiment was forced to give up the red coat. On active service a scarlet flash was worn on the right of the Gurkha hat from the early years of the century. In the Second World War the flash was a flat rectangle with the legend '1 GURKHAS' embroidered in black. Later, the present-day scarlet fold at the top of the hat puggaree was adopted.

THE 2nd KING EDWARD VII'S OWN GURKHA RIFLES (THE SIRMOOR RIFLES)

The Prince of Wales's plumes, crest and motto have been worn as a headdress badge by the 2nd Gurkhas since 1876; that shown is a pattern from the early 20th century. Shown also are two types of shoulder title, and the red-and-black strip of dicing worn on the left side of the Gurkha hat.

The 2nd Gurkhas also trace their origin back to the battalions raised from the Gurkha prisoners of the Nepal War, being raised in Sirmoor in 1815. The Sirmoor Battalion first saw action in the Mahratta War of 1817. In 1825, now called the 8th Local Battalion, they sent 100 men to the siege and capture of Bhurtpore, where they performed with distinction. There followed yet another change of title to the 6th (Sirmoor) Local Battalion before the Battalion's involvement in the First Sikh War, in which the Sirmoors temporarily lost their Regimental Colour at Aliwal, regaining it with a fierce counterattack. The Battalion was also present at Sobraon.

It was at Delhi in 1857, during the Great Mutiny, that the Sirmoor Battalion won fame for itself and established the Gurkha soldiers' courage and loyalty beyond question. On the Hindoo Rao ridge the Sirmoor was under fire for three months and eight days unrelieved, defeating 26 separate attacks and suffering casualties of eight British officers and 327 Gurkhas. On the final capture of Delhi the Sirmoor Battalion was given the honour of garrisoning the Red Fort. In 1858, as official recognition of its services at Delhi, the 'Sirmoor Rifle Regiment' was awarded a third Colour—inscribed 'Delhi' in English, Persian and Hindi—and given the right to carry Colours despite being created a rifle regiment. This privilege was shortlived, and the Colours were removed; in their place Queen Victoria awarded the Regiment the unique distinction of the Truncheon, still carried to this day.

In 1861 the Battalion became, briefly, the 17th Regiment Bengal Native Infantry, before being designated the 2nd Goorkha Regiment, and—in 1864—the 2nd Goorkha (The Sirmoor Rifles) Regiment. In 1876 the Prince of Wales became the Colonel of the Regiment, occasioning yet another change of title to the 2nd (Prince of Wales's Own) Gurkha Regiment (The Sirmoor Rifles). A 2nd Battalion was formed in 1886, winning fame in an action on the Punjab Frontier in 1897 when, in concert with the Gordon Highlanders, they stormed the Dargai Heights. In 1906 the Regiment was re-styled the 2nd King Edward's Own Gurkha Rifles (The Sirmoor Rifles).

During the Great War battalions of the 2nd Gurkhas saw service in France and Egypt (2nd

In the late 1930s the Indian Army adopted the .303 inch Vickers-Berthier light machine gun as a replacement for the Lewis gun. Here, a V-B LMG team of the 10th Gurkhas have rigged an ingenious anti-aircraft mount using rifles and modified bayonets. Note the bugle-and-kukri hat badge; the leather magazine pouches for the LMG slung from the shoulder of the 'number two'; and the '10G' shoulder titles. (Major H. E. Shields)

Battalion) and Mesopotamia (1st Battalion). A third battalion was raised in 1917, serving in India before being disbanded in 1920. In 1936 the brief reign of Edward VIII caused another re-styling of the Regiment to 'King Edward VII's Own'.

Three additional battalions were raised during the Second World War, and served as follows: 1st Battalion—Iraq, Iran, North Africa, Italy and Greece; 2nd Battalion—Malaya, and into Japanese captivity on Singapore Island in February 1942; 3rd Battalion—raised in 1940 and served in Burma, Malaya and Siam; 4th Battalion—raised in 1941 and served in Burma, Indochina and Borneo; 5th Battalion—raised in 1942 and remained in India.

After the war Indian independence led to reconstruction of the battalions: the 3rd was renumbered 2nd in 1946, and the 5th was disbanded. The 1st and 2nd then became part of the British Brigade of Gurkhas, and the 4th became a battalion of the 8th Gurkhas. In the service of Britain the 2nd Gurkhas have seen their full measure of active service, in the Malayan 'emergency' and the 'confrontation' with the Indonesians in Borneo. Garrison duty has included Hong Kong, the present base of Britain's Brigade of Gurkhas.

The full list of the Regiment's battle honours includes: Bhurtpore, Aliwal, Sobraon, Delhi 1857, Kabul 1879, Kandahar 1880, Afghanistan 1878–80, Tirah, Punjab Frontier, La Bassée 1914, Festubert 1914–15, Givenchy 1914, Neuve Chapelle, Aubers, Loos, France and Flanders 1914–15, Egypt 1915, Tigris 1916, Kut-al-Amara 1917, Baghdad, Mesopotamia 1916–18, Persia 1918, Baluchistan 1918, Afghanistan 1919, El Alamein, Mareth, Akarit, Djebel el Meida, Enfidaville, Tunis, North Africa 1942–43, Cassino I, Monastery Hill, Pian di Maggio, Gothic Line, Coriano, Poggio san Giovanni, Monte Reggiano, Italy 1944–45, Greece 1944–45, North Malaya, Jitra, Central Malaya, Kampar, Slim River, Johore, Singapore Island, Malaya 1941–42, North Arakan, Irrawaddy, Magwe, Sittang 1945, Point 1433, Arakan Beaches, Myebon, Tamandu, Chindits 1943, Burma 1942–45.

Dress distinctions of the 2nd Gurkhas include the dicing worn on headdress and the scarlet facings, perpetuated today by the scarlet edging to collars and the scarlet backings to chevrons, cap badges and skill-at-arms badges. The Regiment's lanyard is black.

THE 3rd GORKHA RIFLES

Prior to 1950 the Regiment wore the badge shown at bottom; since then the badge at top has been worn—the old badge featuring the cypher of Queen Alexandra, and the new the lions of Ashoka. At right and left are examples of shoulder titles that have been worn by the Regiment.

The last Gurkha battalion raised in 1815 was recruited from Kumaonis and Garhwals as well as Gurkhas and was called the Kumaon Battalion. For many years it was employed to guard the border with Nepal, becoming the Kumaon Provincial Battalion, the 9th (or Kumaon) Local Battalion, and later being renumbered the 7th. On the outbreak of mutiny in 1857 it was recalled to Delhi, where it took part in the storming of the city.

The Kumaon Battalion was placed in the Bengal Line in 1861 as the 18th Regiment, Bengal Native Infantry, but before the year was out it was to become the 3rd Goorkha Regiment. Subsequent changes of title were the 3rd (The Kumaon) Goorkha Regiment, back to the 3rd Goorkha Regiment, the 3rd Goorkha (Rifle) Regiment in 1891, and the 3rd Gurkha Rifles in 1901.

The 2nd Battalion was raised in 1887 by drafting Garhwalis from other Gurkha battalions. This battalion was redesignated the 39th (The Garhwal) Regiment, Bengal Infantry in 1890, and in the following year a new 2nd Battalion was raised for the

3rd Gurkhas. In 1907 King Edward VII conferred the title of 'Queen's Own' on the Regiment, but at the request of his Queen changed the title to the 3rd Queen Alexandra's Own Gurkha Rifles in 1908.

In the Great War the regular battalions of the Regiment served in Mesopotamia (1st Battalion) and in France, Egypt and Palestine (2nd Battalion). A 3rd Battalion was raised in 1917 in Egypt and was disbanded in 1920. A 4th Battalion was also raised and was disbanded in 1922.

The 3rd and 4th Battalions of the 3rd Gurkhas were again raised in the Second World War, when the battalions served in Burma (1st Battalion); Iraq, Egypt, Cyprus, Palestine and Italy (2nd Battalion); Burma, Malaya and the Dutch East Indies (3rd Battalion); and India (4th Battalion, which was disbanded in 1947).

On the Independence of India the 3rd Gurkhas were allotted to that country, with three battalions in being; 4th and 5th Battalions were raised in 1962 and 1963. With the discarding of the old Imperial titles the Regiment adopted the title of the 3rd Gorkha Rifles and a new badge.

The battle honours of the 3rd Gorkhas are as follows: Delhi 1857, Ahmed Khel, Afghanistan 1878–80, Burma 1885–87, Chitral, Tirah, Punjab Frontier, La Bassée 1914, Armentières 1914, Festubert 1914–15, Givenchy 1914, Neuve Chapelle, Aubers, France and Flanders 1914–15, Egypt 1915–16, Gaza, El Mughar, Nebi Samwil, Jerusalem, Tell-Asur, Megiddo, Sharon, Palestine 1917–18, Sharquat, Mesopotamia 1917–18, Afghanistan 1919, Deir el Shein, North Africa 1940–43, Monte della Gorgace, Il Castello, Monte Farneto, Monte Cavallo, Italy 1943–45, Sittang 1942, Kyaukse 1942, Imphal, Tuitum, Sakawng, Shenam Pass, Bishenpur, Tengnoupal, Meiktila, Defence of Meiktila, Rangoon Road, Pyawbwy, Pegu 1945, Burma 1942–45, Uri, Jammu and Kashmir 1947–48, Shingo River Valley, Jammu and Kashmir 1971.

One of the most distinctive insignia of the 3rd Gurkhas is the dark green triangular patch worn on either side of the Gurkha hat; this appears to have been adopted during the Great War. To this has been added of late a green top fold to the puggaree. Pipers of the Regiment wear Colquhoun tartan, adopted in the 1920s to commemorate the Colquhoun who raised the Kumaon Battalion in 1815.

A medium machine gun platoon of the 10th Gurkhas, Quetta, 1941. The platoon commander is Lieutenant G. O. Whyte, who went on to command 154 (Gurkha) Parachute Battalion. The full equipment of the platoon is on display including guns and tripods, rangefinders and directors. Many of the platoon are armed with pistols and all carry respirators in addition to their '08 pattern fighting order webbing. By this time British officers had adopted the Gurkha hat for wear in the field; previously topees had been worn, which had the effect of making British officers easy to identify. (Major H. E. Shields)

THE 4th GORKHA RIFLES

The present cap badge of the Regiment is shown at centre. It is similar to the badge worn by the 4th from 1924 until 1950, except that the Prince of Wales's crest has been replaced by the lions of Ashoka awarded in recognition of the conduct of the 3rd/4th Gurkhas in 1984 in Kashmir. (The 3rd/4th Gurkhas served with the Chindits in Burma and wear a special breast badge to mark their service.) The badge worn before the 1920s is shown at top right; at top left is the badge worn on the left of the Gurkha hat in the early 20th century. Two types of shoulder title are illustrated: that at left was worn prior to 1890 and that at right by the 1st/4th Gurkhas 1900–1903.

The 4th Gurkhas trace their origins back to 1857 when the Extra Goorkha Regiment was raised to hold the Kumaon Hills after the outbreak of the Great Mutiny. In 1861 the Regiment became the 19th Regiment, Bengal Native Infantry, and subsequently the 4th Goorkha Regiment. Subsequent changes of title were the 4th Gurkha (Rifle) Regiment in 1891, 4th Gurkha Rifles in 1901 and 4th Prince of Wales's Own Gurkha Rifles in 1924.

In 1863 the 4th took part in the Ambeyla Expedition, and the Lushai action in 1871–72. A 2nd Battalion was raised in 1886, both battalions seeing their fair share of active service from that time until 1914, as evidenced by the Regiment's battle honours.

During the Great War the 1st/4th Gurkhas served in France, Gallipoli and Egypt, and the 2nd/4th in Mesopotamia, Salonika and Turkey. A 3rd battalion for the Regiment was raised in 1916 but was posted as the 4th/3rd in error. No errors were made with the 3rd and 4th Battalions raised for the 4th Gurkhas in the Second World War. The 3rd/4th was raised in 1940 and saw service in Burma, the Dutch East Indies and Malaya. The 4th/4th was raised in 1941 and also served in Burma before being disbanded in 1946. The 1st/4th also served in Burma, and the 2nd/4th in Iran, Iraq, Egypt and Italy.

In 1947 the three existing battalions of the 4th Gurkhas were allocated to the Indian Army, becoming, in 1950, the 4th Gorkha Rifles. Further battalions were raised in 1962 (4th), 1963 (5th) and 1970 (6th). Service in the Indian Army has added battle honours to those won in British service: Ali Masjid, Kabul 1879, Kandahar 1880, Afghanistan 1878–80, Waziristan 1895, Chitral, Tirah, Punjab Frontier, China 1900, Givenchy 1914, Neuve Chapelle, Ypres 1915, St. Julien, Aubers, Festubert 1915, France and Flanders 1914–15, Gallipoli 1915, Egypt 1916, Tigris 1916, Kut-al-Amara 1917, Baghdad, Mesopotamia 1916–18, North-West Frontier, India 1917, Balu-

chistan 1918, Afghanistan 1919, Iraq 1941, Syria 1941, The Cauldron, North Africa 1940–43, Trestina, Monte Cedrone, Italy 1943–45, Pegu 1942, Chindits 1944, Mandalay, Burma 1942–45, Gurais, Punch, Jammu and Kashmir 1947–48, Punjab 1965, Jammu and Kashmir 1971.

The first dress of the 4th Gurkhas is recorded as 'Far from uniform. Coats were made from dosuti lined with army blanketing; trousers and pagris were very varied, being supplied by the men themselves.' In more recent times the felt slouch hat was adopted in 1904, and was worn by the 1st/4th Gurkhas with the brim turned up until 1927 (the 1st Battalion also wore topees in the Great War, not discarding them until 1921). All battalions now wear two black folds in the puggaree of their Gurkha hats. At one time the pipers of the 1st/4th wore Black Watch tartan and those of the 2nd/4th that of the HLI. More recently, pipe bags and ribbons have reverted to rifle green.

THE 5th GORKHA RIFLES
(FRONTIER FORCE)

At top centre is the present badge of the 5th, and at bottom centre the badge worn in headdress in the 19th and early 20th centuries. When the 5th became a Royal Regiment they adopted a crown, and then the Royal crest for wear above the numeral 5. After the Royal association was dropped the lions of Ashoka took the place of the crown and lion. At right is the shoulder title

worn until the early 20th century; at left, that worn on becoming a Royal Regiment.

Unlike the other Gurkha regiments, the 5th was not raised within the army of the Bengal Presidency but derived from the old Frontier Force. The 25th Punjab Infantry or Hazara Goorkha Battalion was raised in 1858 with the task of guarding the Hazara frontier. In 1861 the new regiment briefly became the 7th Regiment of Infantry (or Hazara Goorkha Battalion), Punjab Irregular Force, before being renamed as the 5th Goorkha Regiment (or Hazara Goorkha Battalion). Under this name the 5th Gurkhas continued to be attached to the Punjab Irregular Force, which became the Punjab Frontier Force in 1865.

Subsequent changes of title included the 5th Gurkha (Rifle) Regiment in 1891, the 5th Gurkha Rifles in 1901, the 5th Gurkha Rifles (Frontier Force) in 1903, and the 5th Royal Gurkha Rifles (Frontier Force) in 1921. (In 1903, as part of Lord Kitchener's reforms, a single Indian Army was created and the old Punjab Frontier Force ceased to exist. However, its name was carried on in the subsidiary titles of many of the regiments which had formed it.) A 2nd Battalion was raised in 1886.

In the Great War the 1st/5th Gurkhas served in Egypt and Gallipoli and the 2nd/5th in Mesopotamia. A 3rd Battalion was raised in 1916 and also served in Mesopotamia before being disbanded in 1921. In that year the 5th Gurkhas became a Royal regiment, marking the distinction by adopting a scarlet lanyard or shoulder-cord and a crown above the cap badge. This latter was replaced by a lion above a crown in 1927.

The service of the battalions during the Second World War was as follows: 1st Battalion—Iran, Iraq, Egypt and Italy; 2nd Battalion—Burma; 3rd Battalion—Raised in 1940, Burma, Malaya and the Dutch East Indies; 4th Battalion—Raised in 1941, Burma, disbanded in 1946. The 2nd/5th Gurkhas formed part of the Allied force occupying Japan in 1946–47.

In 1947 the three battalions of the 5th Gurkhas were allocated to India, dropping the Royal connection and becoming the 5th Gorkha Rifles (Frontier Force) in 1950. A 4th Battalion was raised in 1963, a 5th Battalion (Chindits) in 1948 by the redesignation of the 3rd/6th Gurkhas, and a 6th Battalion in the same year by the redesignation of the 3rd/7th Gurkhas.

The battle honours of the Regiment are: Peiwar Kotal, Charasiah, Kabul 1879, Kandahar 1880, Afghanistan 1878–80, Punjab Frontier, Helles, Krithia, Suvla, Sari Bair, Gallipoli 1915, Suez Canal, Egypt 1915–16, Khan Baghdadi, Mesopotamia 1916–18, North-West Frontier, India 1917, Afghanistan 1919, North-West Frontier 1930, North-West Frontier 1936–39, The Sangro, Caldari, Cassino II, Sant' Angelo in Teodice, Rocca d'Arce, Rippa Bridge, Femmina Morte, Monte San Bartolo, Italy 1943–45, Sittang 1942, 1945, Kyaukse 1942, Yenangyaung 1942, Stockades, Buthidaung, Imphal, Sakawng, Bishenpur, Shenam Pass, The Irrawaddy, Burma 1942–45, Zoji La, Kargal, Jammu and Kashmir 1947–48, Charwa, Punjab 1965, Shahjra, Sybhat, Punjab 1971, Jammu and Kashmir 1971, East Pakistan 1971.

The long-standing dress distinctions of the 5th Gurkhas are the two green folds in the puggaree of the Gurkha hat, and the scarlet lanyard. The 5th Battalion wear a breast badge to commemorate their service as Chindits. Another distinction was the brown—as opposed to black—'leather' of the 1st/5th, a practice dating back to the brown boots and equipment of the old Frontier Force.

THE 6th QUEEN ELIZABETH'S OWN GURKHA RIFLES

Bottom left is the first badge taken into use by the 6th Gurkhas, and to the right of that the crossed kukris and numeral 6 that replaced it. At top centre is the present badge of the Regiment, flanked to the left by the first shoulder title taken into use, and to the right by the present shoulder title.

The 6th Gurkhas trace their origins back to the Cuttack Legion of 1817, which became the Rangpur Light Infantry Battalion in 1823, the 8th (or Rangpur) Local Light Infantry Battalion in 1826, the 8th (or Assam) Local Light Infantry Battalion in 1828, the 1st Assam Light Infantry in 1844, and the 46th Regiment of Bengal Native Infantry in 1861. In the same year the Regiment was renumbered as the 42nd; it became the 42nd (Assam) Regiment, Bengal Native (Light) Infantry in 1864, dropped the 'Native' from its title in 1885, and in the following year became the 42nd Regiment, Goorkha Light Infantry.

The development into a Gurkha regiment had started in 1818, when the first Gurkhas were enlisted, and was completed by 1886. The sequence of title changes continued in 1889 when the Regiment became the 42nd (Goorkha) Regiment, Bengal (Light) Infantry; the 42nd Gurkha (Rifle) Regiment, Bengal Infantry in 1891; the 42nd Gurkha Rifles in 1901; and the 6th Gurkha Rifles in 1903—a title that the Regiment maintained for 56 years until their present title was bestowed.

The forerunners of the 6th Gurkhas spent most of their time policing the North-East Frontier of India, and fighting the Burma War of 1885–87. The 2nd Battalion was raised in 1904. In the Great War the 1st/6th served in Egypt, Gallipoli and Mesopotamia, and the 2nd/6th in Mesopotamia, Greece and Russia. A 3rd Battalion was raised in 1917, served in India, and was disbanded in 1921. Four battalions saw service in the Second World War: the 1st/6th in Burma; the 2nd/6th in Iraq, Persia, Syria, the Lebanon, Egypt and Italy; the 3rd/6th (raised in 1940) in Burma and Siam; and the 4th/6th (raised in 1941 and disbanded in 1947) in Burma.

In 1947 the 6th Gurkhas were allocated to the British Army, with two battalions (the 3rd went to the 5th Gurkhas). Since that time the Regiment has served and fought in the Far East, although honours for the Malayan and Borneo conflicts have yet to be awarded to add to the list of the battle honours of the 6th Gurkhas:

Burma 1885–87, Helles, Krithia, Suvla, Sari Bair, Gallipoli 1915, Suez Canal, Egypt 1915–16, Khan Baghdadi, Mesopotamia 1916–18, Persia 1918, North-West Frontier, India 1915, Afghanistan 1919, Coriano, Santarcangelo, Monte Chicco, Lamone Crossing, Senio Floodbank, Medicina, Gaiana Crossing, Italy 1944–45, Shwebo, Kyaukmyaung Bridgehead, Mandalay, Fort Dufferin, Maymyo, Rangoon Road, Toungoo, Sittang 1945, Chindits 1944, Burma 1942–45.

The 6th Gurkhas wear very few dress distinctions. The Gurkha hat is worn by the Regiment with a plain puggaree and no badges. A black lanyard is worn, and a commemorative badge, but it may be said that the 6th are distinguished by the plainness of their dress.

THE 7th DUKE OF EDINBURGH'S OWN GURKHA RIFLES

The first badge of the 7th Gurkhas is shown at bottom: a simple design which, like so many badges of the Gurkha regiments, was produced in both white metal and blackened brass. At the top is the present-day badge, which features the coronet and cypher of the Duke of Edinburgh. To the left is the Regiment's first shoulder title, and to the right the present-day version.

In 1902 the 8th Gurkha Rifles were raised, to become in the following year the 2nd Battalion of the 10th Gurkha Rifles. In 1907 this battalion was divided to create 1st and 2nd Battalions of the 7th Gurkha Rifles. This is a simple statement of what was, in fact, a very complicated series of postings and re-musterings of Gurkha troops from disbanded regiments, the Burma Military Police and other Gurkha regiments. Between 1903 and 1907 there had been another 7th Gurkhas, originating from the former 43rd Gurkha Rifles, but this unit became the 8th Gurkha Rifles in 1907 and has no connection with the present 7th.

In the Great War the 1st/7th Gurkhas served in Mesopotamia and the 2nd/7th in Egypt and Mesopotamia. The latter battalion had the misfortune to be part of the garrison of Kut-al-Amara at the time of its capitulation in 1916, and spent the rest of the war in Turkish captivity. A replacement battalion for the 2nd/7th was raised at once. A 3rd Battalion was raised in 1917, serving in India until disbandment in 1921.

During the Second World War the 1st/7th Gurkhas served in Burma and the 2nd/7th in Iran, Iraq, Egypt, Palestine, Italy and Greece. The 2nd/7th were again involved in a capitulation, this time of Tobruk, and were again re-raised. The 3rd/7th Gurkhas were raised in 1940 and fought in Burma before converting to parachute duties, becoming 154 (Gurkha) Parachute Battalion in 1943; this unit was disbanded in 1946. A 4th Battalion was raised in 1941; it served in India and was also disbanded in 1946.

In 1947 the 7th Gurkhas was one of the four regiments chosen for service with Britain's Brigade of Gurkhas. As such, its stations and battles have been those already mentioned. In 1982 the 1st/7th Gurkhas were stationed in the United Kingdom as part of the 5th Infantry Brigade. This was one of the formations chosen to participate in Operation 'Corporate', the retaking of the Falkland Islands in the South Atlantic after the invasion by Argentine forces. The 1st/7th were the only Gurkha unit involved in the Falklands War, and therefore the only British Gurkha unit to be awarded a battle honour since 1945. The full list includes:

Suez Canal, Egypt 1915, Megiddo, Sharon, Palestine 1918, Shaiba, Kut-al-Amara 1915, 1917, Ctesiphon, Baghdad, Sharqat, Mesopotamia 1915–18, Afghanistan 1919, Tobruk 1942, North Africa 1942, Cassino I, Campriano, Poggio del Grillo, Tavoleto, Montebello-Scorticata Ridge, Italy

1944, Pegu 1942, Kyaukse 1942, Shwegyin, Imphal, Bishenpur, Meiktila, Capture of Meiktila, Defence of Meiktila, Rangoon Road, Pyawbwe, Burma 1942–45, Falkland Islands 1982.

The 7th Gurkhas commemorate their affiliation to the former Cameronians (Scottish Rifles) by the wearing of the Douglas tartan by their pipers, and to the Queen's Own Highlanders by the wearing of a patch of Cameron of Erracht tartan on the puggaree of the Gurkha hat, which also has a black top fold. A black and green lanyard is worn.

THE 8th GORKHA RIFLES

The badge of the 8th Gorkhas has undergone no change since its introduction, remaining the simple design shown at centre. A smaller version is used today as a shoulder title, as shown below. The design that preceded it was the 8G shoulder title shown at top right. The 44th Gurkha Rifles, which became the 8th Gurkhas in 1903, wore the numerals 44 (top left) both as cap badge and shoulder title in the late 19th century.

The origins of the 1st/8th Gurkhas can be traced back to 1824 and the raising of the 16th or Sylhet Local Battalion. This became the 11th or Sylhet Local (Light) Infantry Battalion in 1826, and the 48th Regiment, Bengal Native Infantry in 1861; in the same year it was renumbered as the 44th. In 1864 Sylhet and Light Infantry were once more incorporated into the Regiment's title; the 'Native' was

dropped in 1885; and in 1886 it became the 44th Regiment, Goorkha (Light) Infantry. Further changes of title were to the 44th (Goorkha) Regiment, Bengal (Light) Infantry in 1889; the 44th Gurkha (Rifle) Regiment in 1891; and the 44th Gurkha Rifles in 1901. In 1903 it became the 8th Gurkha Rifles, eventually the 1st/8th on being joined by the 2nd Battalion.

The 2nd/8th had an equally complex past, deriving from the Assam Sebundy Corps which was raised in 1835. Subsequent titles were the Lower Assam Sebundy Corps in 1839; the 1st Assam Sebundy Corps later the same year; the 2nd Assam Light Infantry in 1844; and the 47th, renumbered 43rd Regiment, Bengal Native Infantry in 1861. Further changes of title brought in Assam and Light Infantry and dropped 'Native' before, in 1886, the Regiment became the 43rd Regiment, Goorkha Light Infantry. This became the 43rd (Goorkha) Regiment, Bengal (Light) Infantry in 1889; the 43rd Gurkha (Rifle) Regiment, Bengal Infantry in 1891; and the 43rd Gurkha Rifles in 1901. In 1903 the Regiment was renumbered as the 7th Gurkha Rifles and in 1907 became the 2nd Battalion of the 8th Gurkhas.

Much of the early period of the 8th Gurkhas' evolution was spent in the pacification of India's North-Eastern Frontier, the Burma War of 1885–87, and the 1903 expedition to Tibet. At a time when Gurkhas were not eligible for the Victoria Cross, three British officers of the Regiment won the supreme award in 1879, 1891 and 1903.

Three battalions of the 8th Gurkhas served in the Great War: the 1st/8th in Mesopotamia and Egypt, the 2nd/8th in France and Egypt, and the 3rd/8th (raised in 1917 and disbanded in 1921) in India.

Between the World Wars the Indian Army 'kept the peace' in their homeland. History records that in Malabar in 1921 two thousand insurgents attacked a company of the 2nd/8th Gurkhas, actually breaking into their fortification. The 2nd/8th retaliated with kukri and bayonet. When the incident was over 234 insurgents lay dead for the loss of one officer and three Gurkhas.

During the Second World War the 1st/8th Gurkhas saw active service in Burma and the Dutch East Indies; the 2nd/8th served in Iraq, Egypt and Italy. A 3rd Battalion was raised in 1940 and served in

Burma, Indochina and Borneo; and a 4th Battalion, raised in 1941, served in Burma, Siam, Malaya and the Dutch East Indies. The 3rd/8th Gurkhas were disbanded in 1946.

The following year saw the battalions of the 8th Gurkhas allocated to the Indian Army, since when further battalions have been raised—a 5th and a 6th Battalion in 1948 and a 3rd Battalion in 1963. In common with the other Gurkha regiments of the Indian Army, the 8th became 'Gorkha Rifles' in 1949.

The battle honours of the 8th include: Burma 1885–87, La Bassée 1914, Festubert 1914, 1915, Givenchy 1914, Neuve Chapelle, Aubers, France and Flanders 1914–15, Egypt 1915–16, Megiddo, Sharon, Palestine 1918, Tigris 1916, Kut-al-Amara 1917, Baghdad, Mesopotamia 1916–17, Afghanistan 1919, Iraq 1941, North Africa 1940–43, Gothic Line, Coriano, Santarcangelo, Gaiana Crossing, Point 551, Imphal, Tamu Road, Bishenpur, Kanglatongbi, Mandalay, Myinmu Bridgehead, Singhu, Shandat-gyi, Sittang 1945, Burma 1942–45, Punch, Jammu and Kashmir 1947–48, Chushul, Ladakh 1962, San-joi Mirpur, Punjab 1965, Jammu and Kashmir 1965.

A very distinctive item of dress worn by the 8th Gurkhas is the red pompon. This was first worn on the Kilmarnock cap, or bonnet, at a time when most other Gurkha regiments wore a black 'toorie'. With the adoption of the felt slouch hat the pompon/toorie was worn tucked into the puggaree, evolving into the magnificent item worn today.

Gurkhas of one of the battalions of the 43rd Indian Infantry Brigade (2nd/6th, 2nd/8th and 2nd/10th Gurkhas) moving into the line, Italy 1944. Dress and equipment are as in Plate H1. Battalions of all the Gurkha regiments other than the 1st fought in Italy, mostly in unpleasant extremes of climate and terrain and against an enemy who fought a bitter withdrawal.

THE 9th GORKHA RIFLES

The badge of the 9th Gorkhas (top centre) has the lions of Ashoka above the intersection of the kukri blades in place of the crown once worn there in the days of British India. The original badge of the 9th had been as at bottom centre. At left is the original shoulder title of the Regiment, at right the later 9G title.

In lineage terms the 9th Gurkhas claim to be the senior regiment of the eleven now in existence. The 9th traces its origins back to the raising of the Fatehgarh Levy in 1817. This became the Manipuri Levy in 1819, and was brought into the Bengal Line in 1823 as the 32nd Regiment, Bengal Native Infantry. Renumbered the 63rd in 1824, it gained considerable seniority after the Great Mutiny when so many mutinous regiments were disbanded, and the Regiment became the 9th Regiment, Bengal Native Infantry in 1861. It was at this time that the recruitment of a small number of Gurkhas was permitted. The Regiment retained its number throughout subsequent changes of title, becoming the 9th (Gurkha Rifles) Regiment, Bengal Infantry in 1894, and the 9th Gurkha Rifles in 1901. The 9th had become a wholly Gurkha regiment in 1893 and, in 1904, formed into two battalions. The claim of the 9th Gurkhas to senior regiment status stems from the precedence of the 9th Bengal Native Infantry, although Gurkhas were not enlisted until 1861.

During the Great War the 1st Battalion served in France and Mesopotamia, the 2nd Battalion in Mesopotamia. A 3rd Battalion was raised in 1917 and disbanded in 1921 after service in India.

In the Second World War the 1st Battalion served in Iraq, Iran, Egypt, North Africa, Italy and Greece, the 2nd in India, Malaya and Singapore. A 3rd Battalion was raised in 1940 and served in Burma, Malaya and the Dutch East Indies. A 4th Battalion, also raised in 1940, served in Burma, being disbanded in 1947. A 5th Battalion was raised in 1942, served in India, and was redesignated the 2nd Battalion in 1946.

In 1947 the 9th Gurkhas were allocated to India, which re-raised the 4th Battalion in 1961 and the 5th in 1963. The title of the Regiment became the 9th Gorkha Rifles in 1949.

The battle honours of the 9th Gurkhas include: Bhurtpore, Sobraon, Afghanistan 1879–80, Punjab Frontier, La Bassée 1914, Armentières 1914, Festubert 1914, 1915, Givenchy 1914, Neuve Chapelle, Aubers, Loos, France and Flanders 1914–15, Tigris 1916, Kut-al-Amara 1917, Baghdad, Mesopotamia 1916–18, Afghanistan 1919, Djebel el Meida, Djebel Garci, Ragoubet Souissi, North Africa 1940–43, Cassino I, Hangman's Hill, Tavoleto, San Marino, Italy 1943–45, Greece 1944–45, Malaya 1941–42, Chindits 1944, Burma 1942–45, Phillora, Punjab 1965, Derababas Nanak, Kumar Khali, Punjab 1971, Jammu and Kashmir 1971, East Pakistan 1971.

At present the 9th Gurkhas wear a black fold at the top of the Gurkha hat puggaree and a black diamond on the left; the diamond device was first worn by the 2nd/9th in Mesopotamia during the Great War. Both the 3rd and 4th Battalions served with the Chindits and wear the commemorative badge on the left breast.

THE 10th PRINCESS MARY'S OWN GURKHA RIFLES

At top is the Regiment's current badge, worn on the Gurkha hat on a patch of Hunting Stewart tartan. The badge at bottom centre was worn prior to the 1930s on a rifle green patch. At left is the shoulder title with a Roman numeral worn in the 1900s, and at right the present shoulder title.

In 1890 the 10th (Burma) Regiment of Madras Infantry was formed by mustering out the soldiers of

Sharqat, Mesopotamia 1915–18, Afghanistan 1919, Tobruk, 1942, North Africa 1942, Cassino I, Campriano, Poggio del Grillo, Tavoleto, Montebello-Scorticata Ridge, Italy 1944, Sittang 1942, 1945, Pegu 1942, Kyaukse 1942, Shwegyin, Imphal, Bishenpur, Meiktila, Capture of Meiktila, Defence of Meiktila, Rangoon Road, Pyawbwe, Burma 1942–45.

It should be added that the battalions of the 10th Gurkhas are on record as having spent more time in action and having earned more gallantry awards than any other regiment of the Indian Army in the Second World War.

The 10th Gurkhas have worn their cap badge on the right side of the Gurkha hat since the 1920s. At first this was on a patch of rifle green, the shape of which varied according to the battalion; latterly the patch has been of Hunting Stewart tartan, marking the Regiment's affiliation with The Royal Scots (The Royal Regiment). The Regiment wears a black lanyard, and an elephant and rock fort badge on the left arm to commemorate the battles of Assaye and Amboor.

THE 11th GORKHA RIFLES

The present-day badge of the 11th Gorkhas is at top centre. At bottom right is a 'slip-on' shoulder title of the Regiment as worn in the late 1940s. The badge of the 11th Gurkhas raised in 1918 was a plain crossed kukri design with no numerals.

the 10th Madras Infantry and posting in men from the Kubo Valley Military Police, mostly Gurkhas. The Regiment soon became wholly Gurkha in composition, changing title to become the 10th Regiment (1st Burma Rifles), Madras Infantry in 1892; the 10th Regiment (1st Burma Gurkha Rifles), Madras Infantry in 1895; and the 10th Gurkha Rifles in 1901. In 1903 a 2nd Battalion was raised, which was used to form the two battalions of the 7th Gurkhas in 1907; in 1908 a new 2nd Battalion of the 10th Gurkhas was raised.

During the Great War the 1st Battalion served in Mesopotamia, and the 2nd in Egypt, Gallipoli and Mesopotamia. The Second World War took them to Burma (1st Battalion), and Iraq, Syria, Iran and Italy (2nd Battalion). A 3rd Battalion was raised in 1940 and served in Burma, Malaya and the Dutch East Indies before being disbanded in 1947. A 4th Battalion was raised in 1941 and served in Burma, Indochina and Cambodia.

In 1947 the Regiment was allocated to the British Army with its 1st and 2nd Battalions. In 1949 it became the 10th Princess Mary's Own Gurkha Rifles.

The battle honours of the Regiment include: Amboor, Carnatic, Mysore, Assaye, Ava, Burma 1885–87, Suez Canal, Egypt 1915, Megiddo, Sharon, Palestine 1918, Shaiba, Kut-al-Amara 1915, 1917, Ctesiphon, Defence of Kut-al-Amara, Baghdad,

The first 11th Gurkhas were raised during the last year of the Great War. At the time British troops were desperately needed on the Western Front and, with reserves at home almost exhausted, units were drafted from the Middle East. Their places were taken by units of the Indian Army, and an 11th Regiment of Gurkha Rifles was created in the Middle East to provide extra battalions. The 1st/11th Gurkhas was raised from companies drawn from existing battalions of the 5th and 6th Gurkhas; the 2nd/11th from companies of the 2nd, 3rd, 4th and 7th Gurkhas; the 3rd/11th from companies of the 9th and 10th Gurkhas and the 1st and 2nd Battalions, 39th Garhwal Rifles; and the 4th/11th from companies of

the 1st, 3rd and 7th Gurkhas. All these battalions of the 11th Gurkhas were disbanded between 1919 and 1922. The only battle honour recorded for the 11th is that for Afghanistan 1919.

No 11th Gurkhas were raised in the Second World War, extra battalions of the existing regiments being considered sufficient. In 1948, however, the Indian Army began forming battalions of a new 11th Gurkha Rifles (11th Gorkha Rifles from 1949) from the 'surplus' battalions of the British Gurkha regiments. In all four battalions were formed in that year, a 5th in 1952, a 6th and a 7th in 1964.

The battle honours of the Regiment are all post-Independence, and include: Bogra, Shingo River

Subedar Bombahadur Rai of the 4th/10th Gurkhas smiles as he displays Japanese swords captured at Wainggyo, Burma, 1944. The 4th Battalion wore a triangular patch of rifle green on the puggaree of their Gurkha hats. (Major H. E. Shields)

Valley, Jammu and Kashmir 1971, East Pakistan 1971.

Photographs of individuals taken shortly after the Regiment's formation show the only dress distinction to have been a black lanyard. Since then the 11th Gurkhas have adopted a crimson fold in the top of the Gurkha hat puggaree and crimson badge backing.

THE GURKHA PARACHUTE UNITS

The first Gurkha parachute troops wore the Gurkha hat with a light blue patch on the left of the puggaree bearing a parachute above crossed kukris. 153 (Gurkha) Parachute Battalion adopted kukris with the edges downwards, as at top left; 154 (Gurkha) Parachute Battalion had the edges upwards, as at top right. The devices were embroidered in white. The badges were also made in white metal—see top centre, 153 (Gurkha) Parachute Battalion. When the Indian Parachute Regiment was created in 1945 the Gurkhas took into wear the maroon beret on which was worn the badge of the British Parachute Regiment, inscribed 'India'. The Gurkha Independent Parachute Company of the 1960s also wore the maroon beret; the badge of the Parachute Regiment was worn on a patch of rifle green with two strips of Brigade of Gurkhas ribbon—see below.

During the Second World War the British raised a large number of airborne units, and training organisations existed in Britain, the Middle East and India. The British system operated by calling for volunteers for parachute duties, and also by converting units as a group. The two Gurkha parachute battalions raised in India are a good example of both methods. 153 (Gurkha) Parachute Battalion was raised in 1941 from volunteers from all the Gurkha regiments; 154 (Gurkha) Parachute Battalion, which was raised in the following year, was formed by 'converting' the 3rd/7th Gurkhas.

The two units became part of an airborne organisation in India that developed into divisional strength. The 2nd Indian Airborne Division—previously the 44th—was intended to spearhead the recapture of Malaya from the Japanese. It never saw action, as the dropping of the atomic bombs on Hiroshima and Nagasaki put an abrupt end to the Far East war.

Prior to the formation of the 44th Indian Airborne Division the Gurkha Parachute Battalions existed as part of the 50th Indian Parachute Brigade, which had been formed in October 1941 with one British (151), one Indian (152) and one Gurkha (153) parachute battalions in addition to the usual command, pathfinder, signal, support weapons, sapper and medical sub-units. An Air Landing School was established and training commenced, using elderly Vickers Valentia aircraft. Over the course of many months the men of the Brigade qualified in the parachute role, and settled down to a routine of exercises and hard training to equip themselves for the battles ahead. In time better equipment and better aircraft (C-47 Dakotas) became available, and efficiency rose. When 151 (British) Parachute Battalion was sent to the Middle East, its place was taken by 154 (Gurkha) Parachute Battalion, leaving the fighting element of the Brigade heavily loaded towards the Gurkhas.

In time the 50th Indian Parachute Brigade had the soul-destroying experience of sitting out the air-landing phase of the second Chindit expedition after converting to the infantry role prior to their entry into the Burma campaign. In March 1944 the Brigade held the Sangshak position in front of Imphal when a thrust of the Japanese offensive broke against it. In savage fighting the Japanese were held and eventually forced to withdraw. In time the Brigade withdrew to India to retrain in the parachute role.

Finally, in early 1945, came the opportunity for parachute operations; and a battalion group consisting of elements of both Gurkha battalions—soon to be retitled the 2nd and 3rd (Gurkha) Battalions, the Indian Parachute Regiment—parachuted on 1 May to seize Elephant Point to safeguard part of the assault on Rangoon.

Although preparation for the planned attack on Malaya continued, the fighting days of the Gurkha parachute battalions were over. The 2nd carried on until 1947 before being disbanded, and the 3rd was converted back to the 3rd/7th Gurkhas in 1946.

India maintained parachute forces after 1947, and formed a new Parachute Regiment in the early 1950s. At first Gurkhas were posted to form part of the Regiment's 2nd Battalion, but since 1961 they have formed part of the 4th Battalion. Gurkhas have also formed part of the 8th Battalion, raised in 1965. Thus the Indian Army has kept no all-Gurkha parachute units, but has maintained Gurkha parachute sub-units as part of its Parachute Regiment, the battle honours of which are:

Keren, Berbera, Abyssinia 1940–41, British Somaliland 1940, Mersa Matruh, North Africa 1940–43, Monte della Gordace, Il Castello, Pratelle Pass, San Martino Sogliano, Monte Farneto, Monte Cavallo, Idice Bridgehead, Italy 1943–45, The Shweli, Magwe, Kama, Sittang 1945, Burma 1942–45, Srinagar, Naushera, Jhanger, Punch, Jammu and Kashmir 1947–48, Hajipur, Jammu and Kashmir 1965, Defence of Punch, Chachro, Poongli Bridge, Sindh 1971, East Pakistan 1971.

The first Gurkha 'paras' wore no special devices other than Indian-made wings and a puggaree badge of a parachute over crossed kukris. Later the maroon beret was adopted, and this was continued after 1947.

A **Gurkha Independent Parachute Company** was formed from Britain's Brigade of Gurkhas in the early 1960s and was in existence for about 10 years. It was formed in Malaya from personnel of the 1st/10th, 2nd/10th and 1st/7th Gurkhas, and trained at the parachute training centre at Changi, Singapore.

Two riflemen of the 1st/10th Gurkhas, Burma, 1944. Note the black cat divisional sign of the 17th Indian Infantry Division worn on both sleeves by the man at left. (Major H. E. Shields)

During the Borneo 'confrontation' with Indonesia the Gurkha Independent Parachute Company was reported as having operated with the 22nd Special Air Service Regiment, patrolling the 700-mile border with Indonesian territory; however, little has been recorded of this. In the raising, training and leading of a local force known as the Border Scouts the Gurkha 'paras' played a leading role. They maintained their parachute capability throughout the confrontation, but it is unlikely that the Gurkhas undertook a parachute insertion into battle during the war with Indonesia.

Men serving with the Gurkha Independent Parachute Company wore the maroon beret with the badge of Britain's Parachute Regiment, parachute qualification wings, and a shoulder title 'GURKHA'.

THE QUEEN'S GURKHA ENGINEERS

Two Kukris in saltire, the blades upwards and outwards, in silver ensigned with a grenade and over the pommels a scroll inscribed 'Ubique' in gold: so runs the heraldic designation of the badge of the Queen's Gurkha Engineers—above. A shoulder title QGE in blackened metal is worn, as is a blue lanyard.

Gurkhas were first enlisted into Britain's Royal Engineers in 1948 when 67 Field Squadron RE was formed in Malaya. In 1950 a second Gurkha squadron, 68 Field Squadron RE, was formed; and a regimental headquarters, 50 Field Engineer Regiment RE, in Hong Kong in 1951. 50 Field Regiment was incorporated into the Brigade of Gurkhas in 1955, its designation being changed to the Gurkha Engineers. Subsequently two more squadrons were raised: 69 Gurkha Field Squadron and 70 Gurkha Field Park Squadron. In 1977 the Regiment became the Queen's Gurkha Engineers.

In recent times Britain's defence cutbacks have periodically reduced the strength of the Brigade of Gurkhas, and the Queen's Gurkha Engineers have not escaped the Ministry of Defence axe. Reduced to two squadrons, based in Hong Kong, they face the uncertain future that seems to be the fate of all Britain's Gurkhas.

THE QUEEN'S GURKHA SIGNALS

In front of the figure of Mercury on a globe in silver, ensigned by and supporting in his dexter hand, the Crown in gold, two kukris in saltire, the blades upwards and inwards, also in silver, thereunder a scroll inscribed 'Certa Cito' also in gold.

There had long been Gurkhas trained in the arts of signalling before the formation in 1950 of what was to become the Gurkha Divisional Signal Regiment; but these had been unit signallers, responsible for communications within battalions. The proposed formation of a Gurkha division by the British called for the appropriate divisional communications units, and the first Gurkhas began training. By 1953 one independent brigade squadron and three brigade signal troops had been formed, and in October of that year 17 Gurkha Divisional Signal Regiment came into being. Until 1955 these units were part of the Royal Corps of Signals, but in that year were incorporated into the Brigade of Gurkhas with the title Gurkha Signals. In 1977 this became the Queen's Gurkha Signals. Like the Gurkha sappers the Gurkha signallers have been reduced since the days of the Gurkha Division, and are now in Hong Kong.

THE GURKHA TRANSPORT REGIMENT

On an eight-pointed Star in silver a Scroll inscribed 'Gurkha Transport Regiment'. Issuant therefrom a wreath of laurel, all in gold, over all, two Kukris in saltire, also in silver handled gold, ensigned with the Royal Cypher also in gold.

Raised as the Gurkha Army Service Corps in 1958, the Regiment comprised two companies, Number 28 and Number 30, the personnel of which were volunteers from the Gurkha infantry battalions. Within a year the Regiment had acquired the title of the Gurkha Transport Regiment, had grown to four companies, and had been incorporated into the Brigade of Gurkhas. The Regiment, reduced from its peak establishment, is now based in Hong Kong.

GURKHA PROVOST

A Provost Company was raised in 1949 from British and Gurkha personnel, and this in time became 17 Gurkha Divisional Provost Company, Gurkha Military Police. A unit entitled No. 5 (Gurkha) Dog Company, Gurkha Military Police was formed from the Divisional Provost Company. Both have now been disbanded.

Other British Gurkha Units

Within the British Brigade of Gurkhas since 1948 various units have been formed which, for one reason or another, were shortlived. The planners of 17 Gurkha Division decreed that the Division's artillery would be manned by Gurkhas, and called for the formation of three Gurkha field regiments, one Gurkha anti-aircraft regiment and one Gurkha anti-tank regiment. In Malaya early in 1948 the 1st and 2nd Battalions of the 7th Gurkhas began training as gunners and were designated the 101st and 102nd Field Regiments, Royal Artillery. In the event the training was conducted in a war zone, as the 'emergency' had broken out at the same time as the 7th Gurkhas were being introduced to their 25-pounders. As the Malayan war developed it called for many more infantry units than were available, and so the erstwhile Gurkha gunners reverted to their infantry role immediately, and to their infantry titles in the following year.

The planners also envisaged a role for ordnance, electrical and mechanical engineer, and catering units all manned by Gurkha personnel; and in 1950 recruits were enlisted in Nepal and trained in Malaya for these roles. However, the units were never formed and the personnel for them were posted to Gurkha infantry regiments.

In 1955 a staff band for the Brigade of Gurkhas was formed on the existing band of the 2nd Gurkhas.

In 1960 training aimed at the formation of a Gurkha unit of the Royal Army Medical Corps began; the personnel were serving Gurkhas who had already received training as unit medical staff. This initiative also came to naught, and a Gurkha RAMC unit was never formed.

The British Army has a long-standing tradition of enlisting boys, and in 1948 it established a training company in Malaya for Gurkha boys. The unit was in

Until 1912 only British officers of the Gurkha regiments were eligible for the Victoria Cross. Gurkha officers and men had been rewarded by the Indian Order of Merit for gallantry. King George V's order of 1912 made all officers and men of the Indian Army eligible for the supreme award.

Lt. J. A. Tytler, Bengal Staff Corps, serving with 66th Bengal Native Infantry; Indian Mutiny, 10 February 1858.
Maj. D. MacIntyre, Bengal Staff Corps, serving with 2nd GR; Lushai Campaign, 4 January 1872.
Brevet Maj. G. N. Channer, Bengal Staff Corps, serving with 1st GR; Malaya, 20 December 1875.
Capt. J. Cook, Bengal Staff Corps, serving with 5th GR; Afghanistan, 2 December 1878.
Capt. R. K. Ridgeway, Bengal Staff Corps, serving with 44th GR; Nagar Campaign, 22 November 1879.
Lt. C. J. W. Grant, Indian Staff Corps, serving with 12th Burma Regt.; Manipur, 27 March 1891.
Lt. G. H. Boisragon, 5th GR; Hunza Campaign, 2 December 1891.
Lt. J. Manners-Smith, Indian Staff Corps, serving with 5th GR; Hunza Campaign, 20 December 1891.
Capt. W. G. Walker, 1/4th GR; Somaliland, 22 April 1903.
Lt. J. D. Grant, 1/8th GR; Tibet, 6 July 1904.

Rfm. Kulbir Thapa, 2/3rd GR; France, 25 September 1915.
Maj. G. C. Wheeler, 2/9th GR; Mesopotamia, 23 February 1917.
Rfm. Karnabahadur Rana, 2/3rd GR; Egypt, 10 April 1918.
Subedar Lalbahadur Thapa, 1/2nd GR; Tunisia, 5/6 April 1943.
Havildar Gaje Ghale, 2/5th RGR; Burma, 24–27 May 1944.
A/Capt. M. Allmand, RAC attached to 6th GR; Burma, 11–23 June 1944.
Rfm. Ganju Lama, 1/7th GR; Burma, 12 June 1944.
Rfm. Tulbahadur Pun, 3/6th GR; Burma, 23 June 1944.
Rfm. Agansing Rai, 5th RGR; Burma, 24–25 June 1944.
A/Subedar Netrabahadur Thapa, 2/5th RGR; Burma, 25–26 June 1944.
T/Maj. F. G. Blaker, HLI attached to 3/9th GR; Burma, 9 July 1944.
Rfm. Sherbahadur Thapa, 1/9th GR; Italy, 18 September 1944.
Rfm. Thaman Gurung, 1/5th RGR; Italy, 19 November 1944.
Rfm. Bhanbagta Gurung, 3/2nd GR; Burma, 5 March 1945.
Rfm. Lachhman Gurung, 4/8th GR; Burma, 12 May 1945.
L/C Rambahadur Limbu, 2/10th GR; Borneo, 21 November 1965.

existence for many years but was dispensed with in the 1960s.

The Royal Nepalese Army

Nepal necessarily maintains armed forces, into which the Gurkhas enlist. Many of the regiments of the Royal Nepalese Army have lineages going back before the formation of the British India Gurkhas, and count amongst their battle honours the wars against the British. Conversely, many show honours for service alongside the British at the time of the Indian Mutiny and during both World Wars.

The senior unit is the Sri Nath Battalion, raised in 1763. The Purano Gorakh Battalion was also raised in 1763 as the First Gurkha Company and, like the Sri Nath, has an impressive record of service, first against the British and later alongside them. The Kali Bahadur Battalion was raised in 1831, and was the first Nepalese unit to fight 'overseas' in Burma in the Second World War. Other units from Nepal include the Sher, the Mahindra Dal, the Shamsher Dal, the First Rifles, the Devi Dutt and the Gorakh Bahadur.

UNIFORM AND RANKS

The Indian Army of the British Raj maintained a distinctive uniform style for much of its history. This style mirrored the native dress dictated by custom, religion and climate, and manifested itself particularly in the many patterns of headdress worn by regiments and castes.

The Gurkhas departed early from native dress and soon adopted a uniform of European style. By the late 19th century this had developed into the rifle green uniform and black pill-box cap worn on occasions to this day.

The Indian Army was the first to adopt khaki for field service and, as part of that army, the Gurkhas soon utilised this practical colour and style of dress. Less practical was the pillbox or Kilmarnock cap, and this was replaced by the felt slouch hat in the early 20th century—since when, worn in a distinctive style, it has become a symbol of the fighting Gurkha.

A more famous and more obvious symbol is the traditional weapon of the Gurkha soldier, the kukri knife. Carried on the right hip, the kukri has, down the years, required some modifications of equipment geometry to accommodate it. The weapon has given

The kukri fighting knife has been the weapon of the Gurkha soldier for centuries. Designed for cutting—as opposed to thrusting—the kukri of the World Wars is about 17 inches overall with a blade length of about 13 inches. The weapon illustrated is of Great War vintage and has walnut grips and a wooden scabbard covered in leather; the scabbard has a metal chape and a leather frog. Contained in the scabbard are a small knife and a sharpening steel. The kukri of the early 19th century was somewhat larger than that illustrated, and that currently carried is smaller, with a blade length of about 11 inches. An item of dress that the Gurkhas have made their own is the felt or Gurkha hat. In reality this is two hats; the larger has the lining removed, the smaller is fitted inside, and the brims are sewn together. The crown is then folded fore-and-aft, a turban or puggaree is wound on and a chinstrap added. The hat illustrated is that of the 1st Gurkhas of about 1945; the puggaree patch is red and the lettering black.

rise to an enormous amount of blarney regarding its use. (The author recalls being told hair-raising stories of the use of the kukri in the trenches in the Great War. He was six years old, and the storyteller was his grandfather. He was to hear the stories repeated many times and in many contexts, but they always featured Gurkhas moving silently into the enemy trenches to bring back various parts of corpses as evidence of their prowess with the kukri.)

The truth is that the kukri has been used as a close-quarters weapon on many recorded occasions, and with great success and efficiency. However, Gurkhas are not required to draw blood each time

Lance-naik Kharkabahadur Tamang of the 3rd/10th Gurkhas wearing the ribbon of the Military Medal he won in Java in November 1945. Note the diamond-shaped patch of rifle green worn behind the badge in his general service cap, the distinction of the 3rd Battalion. (Major H. E. Shields)

they draw their kukris. (The story was legend that in order to satisfy this requirement a Gurkha would nick his thumb if he ever drew his kukri to show it to a British soldier.) Equally, the kukri is as much a tool as a weapon. The author recalls watching the demonstration platoon of Gurkhas at the Far East training centre putting up a fence with their kukris: the knives were used to clear the undergrowth, dig post-holes, cut timber, and even to hammer in the nails. To this end those particular Gurkhas had one working kukri, and one highly polished and mounted one for ceremonial laid out on their kits in the barracks.

The rank structure of the Gurkha Regiments is worth a mention. For years this followed the practices of the Indian Army, and for non-commissioned ranks was thus:

British Army equivalent	Indian rank
Private	Sepoy/Rifleman
Lance-Corporal	Lance-Naik
Corporal	Naik
Sergeant	Havildar

Indian NCOs wore the same badges of rank as their British counterparts, and the ranks above Sergeant all had their equivalent up to Battalion Havildar Major. After India's independence the British Gurkhas adopted non-commissioned ranks in English.

Commissioned ranks in the Indian Army were more complicated. British officers received their commissions from the Sovereign, as did a number of Indians from 1918 onwards. However, there was a long-standing practice of Indian Officers (IOs) who were, in reality, NCOs promoted for their experience and long service. Their grades were Jemedar (one star), Subedar (two stars), and Subedar-Major (crown).

During the Second World War the badges of rank of these Viceroy Commissioned Oficers (VCOs)—as they had become in the 1930s—were changed to smaller stars on bands of red-yellow-red ribbon. Subedar-Majors were ordered to wear three small crowns on bands of ribbon. In 1945 there was a reversion to the former badges of rank, but with a single band of ribbon. After partition this system was maintained for Indian Army Gurkhas, but with different badges replacing stars and crowns.

In the British Gurkha regiments the VCOs became King's Gurkha Officers (KGOs), and later Queen's Gurkha Officers (QGOs). Their badges are: Lieutenant (QGO), two stars; Captain (QGO), three stars; and Major (QGO), a crown, all worn on a strip of ribbon in the green, red and black colours of the Brigade of Gurkhas.

THE PLATES

A: The Early Years
Very little pictorial evidence survives to show the dress and equipment of the Gurkhas at the time of their war with the British, 1814–16. The figure at **A1** is taken from a surviving painting of a group of

Early years:
1: Goorkha warrior, 1815
2: Gurkha sepoy, 1816
3: Sepoy, 1st Nasiri Battalion, 1820s

A

The Sirmoor Battalion (later 2nd Gurkhas), Delhi 1857:
1: Sepoy
2: British officer
3: Naik

1: Bugler, 4th Gurkhas, 1880s
2: British Lieutenant,
   4th Gurkhas, early 1900s
3: Lt. Col., 8th Gurkhas, early 1900s
4: Piper, 5th Gurkhas, 1890s
5: Subedar, 1st Gurkhas, 1880s

C

The Western Front, 1915:
1: Rifleman (V.C. winner), 3rd Gurkhas
2: British Captain, 1st Gurkhas
3: Rifleman, 1st Gurkhas

The Middle East:
1: Rifleman, 3rd Gurkhas, 1917
2: Lance-Naik, 5th Gurkhas, 1918
3: Rifleman, 10th Gurkhas, 1915

E

1: Rifleman, 8th Gurkhas, 1920s
2: Piper, 10th Gurkhas, 1930s
3: Havildar, 9th Gurkhas, 1930s

North-West Frontier of India, 1930s
1: Havildar, 2/4th Gurkhas
2: Lance-Naik, 3rd Gurkhas
3: Naik, 5th Royal Gurkhas
4: Signaller, 2/4th Gurkhas

Italy, 1944/45:
1: Havildar, 6th Gurkhas
2: Rifleman
3: British Major, 3rd Gurkhas

H

The Far East:
1: Naik, 9th Gurkhas, 1941/42
2: Rifleman, 1945
3: Subedar, Gurkha Parachute Battalion, 1945

I

1: Lieutenant (QGO), 2nd Gurkhas, 1970s
2: Rifleman, 7th Gurkhas, 1950s
3: British officer, 6th Gurkhas, 1950s

1: Lance-Naik, 5th Gurkhas, 1960s
2: Junior NCO, Nepal Army, 1970s
3: Lance-corporal (V.C. winner), 10th Gurkhas, 1960s

1: Lieutenant (QGO), 6th Gurkhas, 1990s
2: NCO, 8th Gurkhas, 1990s
3: Rifleman, 7th Gurkhas, 1982

Gurkha soldiers, or warriors, of this time, and shows their dress to have been similar to the native Nepalese garments worn well into the 20th century. Common to all Gurkha warriors was the kukri knife, similar in shape and design to the contemporary weapon but somewhat larger. Firearms were carried by some Gurkha warriors of 1814–16, but a number were armed as the figure depicted, with a sword and a circular shield. Note the helmet worn over the puggaree, or headcloth, and the beads worn at the throat.

The sepoy, A2, shows one of the first uniforms worn by Gurkhas in the British service. Details are, once again, taken from a contemporary painting and show a transition from native to European dress, the puggaree, trousers and footwear all being local items. The kukri was still being worn in front of the body in a cummerbund sash, and was still of larger size than that of today. Crossbelts support an ammunition pouch and a bayonet, and the musket appears to be a cut-down version of the India pattern of the time. Note the cross belt plate, from which hang the picker and brush necessary for the cleaning of the frizzen and pan of the musket. The appearance of an early move towards rifle regiment garb is also obvious.

By the 1820s the 1st Nasiri Battalion had adopted a uniform much more similar to that of a British rifle regiment, as worn by the sepoy at A3. The bell-topped shako had replaced the puggaree, and European-style trousers and boots were worn. The kukri was by now worn from a waist belt, over the right hip, where it must have interfered with access to the pouch. The musket and bayonet are the India pattern, and the kukri is still of the original large pattern. Details for this figure are taken from a contemporary painting.

B: The Sirmoor Battalion, Delhi, 1857

Mention has already been made of the glorious exploits of the Sirmoor Battalion (later the 2nd

Many formation signs have been worn by the Gurkhas, but those illustrated are of particular interest. At left is that of the 43rd Indian Infantry Brigade, the 'Gurkha lorried infantry'; the sign—white kukris on a rifle green field—was first worn in Italy in 1945, and later became that of the 17th Gurkha Division in Malaya. The same sign was worn with a red field by 48 Gurkha Infantry Brigade, a black field by 63 Gurkha Infantry Brigade, and a brown field by 99 Gurkha Infantry Brigade. In the 1960s 17 Gurkha Division wore the black cat of the old 17th Indian Infantry Division, shown at right, on a yellow ground. The sign was frequently worn on the right sleeve with the brigade sign on the left. The sign of the original 17 Division was a lightning flash, but this was replaced by the cat in 1943. In its first form a khaki field was used. Illustrated at centre is the formation sign worn in 1945 by the Indian Airborne Division and by the two Gurkha parachute battalions who were part of it.

Gurkhas) during the mutiny of 1857, and in particular their conduct at the siege of Delhi. The figures on this plate depict the dress of the men of the battalion at that time, the details taken from a number of contemporary paintings and photographs. Other ranks appear to have worn a 'cocked' version of the Kilmarnock bonnet with red-and-black dicing and a bugle-horn badge. Not only the rifle green uniform marked the Sirmoor as a rifle unit; they had for some time been armed with a pattern of the Brunswick rifle. The kukri was by now worn forward of the cartridge pouch, but must still have interfered with access to ammunition. A cap pouch was worn on the waist belt, as was the bayonet in a frog. **B1** shows a sepoy ramming down a cartridge, while **B3** shows a naik about to fire his rifle.

The British officer of the Sirmoor at **B2** is shown in the hot-weather dress of the battalion, which featured a white 'Havelock' cap cover and white cotton trousers. Note his pouch belt with whistle and chain, black sash, and sword belt for his 1845-pattern sword.

At the siege of Delhi the Sirmoor Battalion served alongside the British 60th Rifles (later the King's Royal Rifle Corps), beginning an association that was to lead to the adoption by the 2nd Gurkhas of many of the KRRC dress distinctions, including the scarlet facings worn to this day. Also still worn are the red-and-black dicing on headdress. The conduct of the Gurkha regiments during the Mutiny, their loyalty,

▼ *Men of B Company, 2nd/10th Gurkhas who participated in an ambush at Bukit Siput, Malaya, in 1957. All five of the Communist terrorists (CTs) contacted were killed—in the parlance of the time a 100% kill-to-contact, and a remarkable achievement. Corporal Jitbahadur Rai (kneeling, left) killed three himself and was awarded the Military Medal. All carry the 9mm L2 Sterling sub-machine gun. (Major H. E. Shields)*

▶ *General Sir Gerald Templer contratulates men of a platoon of the 2nd/10th Gurkhas after an action in which they had killed six and captured three of the 35 CTs contacted; Malaya, 1950s. The battle was a result of the pursuit of the terrorists after they had attacked a party of policemen. Successful 'follow-ups' called for speed in reaction and movement. (Major H. E. Shields)*

steadfastness and fighting spirit did much to promote their reputation in official circles, and led to the expansion of Gurkha units in the reformation of the Indian Army after the Mutiny.

The background shows one of the many gates to the walled city of Delhi at the time of the siege.

C: The High Noon of Empire

The period between the suppression of the Mutiny in 1858 and the outbreak of the Great War in 1914 saw much reform of the Indian Army. The Kitchener reforms of the early 1900s saw ten regiments of Gurkhas brought into what was termed the Gurkha 'Line', with each regiment comprising two battalions. The Line was to remain in this form—with the exception of war-raised units—until Indian Independence in 1947. The figures on this plate depict some of the varieties of uniform worn between 1857 and 1914.

At **C1** is a bugler of the 4th Gurkhas in the 1880s, dressed for field service in khaki cotton drill, his uniform featuring leggings and cap-cover with a wide, wired brim. The only insignia worn by rank and file with this uniform was the numeral '4' on the shoulder straps. Equipment of the time was the brown leather belt and braces adopted by the Indian Army and worn with pouches and a waterbottle and haversack. Note the kukri, still of quite large dimensions, and the 'silver' bugle of a rifle regiment.

At **C2** is a British officer of the 4th Gurkhas, depicted in the field service dress of the early 1900s. His uniform comprises a 'Cawnpore topee' pith helmet, khaki drill shirt and shorts and puttees. His equipment is what is described in the regimental history of the 4th Gurkhas as 'Christmas Tree order'!—basically, the Sam Browne belt and braces with pistol, pouch, binoculars and haversack. Worn

Corporal, 6th Gurkhas, Malaya 1950s: a painting by the present author, who served in Malaya 1953–55 with the 1st Battalion, Royal Hampshire Regiment. Like most British soldiers at the time, the author met Gurkha troops both on and off duty and shared the general high opinion of their behaviour, bearing and turnout. It is a simple statement of fact that no other troops in the Far East came close to the Gurkhas when 'turned-out' for a parade. Note the board-like starching of the uniform, the black hosetops now in use, the loose sling of a rifle regiment, and the general appearance that bespeaks pride in Regiment and in self. The weapon is a .303 inch No. 5 rifle.

The Pipes and Drums of the 1st/7th Gurkhas at Kuang, Malaya, 1956. The white uniforms were a Gurkha version of the British Army's No. 3 dress—a tropical ceremonial uniform. Only the Gurkhas wore shorts with this uniform. (Ray Gipson)

with this are a rucksack, and a megaphone on a lanyard; yet another lanyard secures his Webley .455 inch revolver. Shorts, 'Janghirs' in Hindustani, were adopted in India at about this time, the Gurkhas being among the first to do so.

In contrast, **C3** depicts a lieutenant-colonel of the 5th Gurkhas in the full dress of the early 1900s. His uniform is exactly that of an officer of a British rifle regiment except for the helmet and regimental insignia. These include a red 'tuft' in the helmet, a pouch belt badge, and the regimental bit, brow band and throat ornament on the horse furniture.

During this period many Gurkha regiments raised pipe bands, instruction coming from the pipers of the many Scottish regiments stationed in India; and **C4** shows a piper of the 5th Gurkhas in the 1890s. His uniform includes a jacket cut in the style of a Scottish tunic, Scottish 'spats', a Glengarry bonnet and a fly plaid. The tartan of the plaid, pipe bag and ribbons is the 'Universal' or Black Watch used by many regiments at the time. Note the black-cock's feathers in his bonnet, cap badge, plaid brooch, and the waist belt which supports a kukri on his right hip.

Figure **C5** depicts a subedar of the 1st Gurkhas in the 1880s, just before the Regiment adopted rifle green dress in place of the red coat. The rank badge of a subedar in a Gurkha regiment at this time was crossed kukris; jemedars wore a single kukri badge. The general appearance of this officer is that of a light infantryman as opposed to a rifleman; this reflects the title of the time, the 1st Goorkha Regiment (Light Infantry). Note the pouch belt, whistle and chain, 1845-pattern 'Gothic hilt' sword, sling belt, and cap insignia of a bugle-horn and the numeral '1'. (Sources: photographs, drawings, regimental histories, dress regulations.)

D: The Western Front, 1915

On the outbreak of war in 1914 Britain sent her 'contemptible little army' (the British Expeditionary Force) to France, where it sustained grievous casualties in the opening battles of the war. Amongst the first reinforcements for the BEF were Indian Army formations, which included battalions from several of the Gurkha regiments. The figures on this

plate represent the typical appearance of the Gurkhas who fought in the trenches of Flanders at that time.

Figure **D1** depicts Rifleman Kulbir Thapa of the 2nd Battalion, 3rd Queen Alexandra's Own Gurkha Rifles, who won the Victoria Cross on 25 September 1915. During an attack on the German trenches during which he himself was wounded, he found a badly wounded British soldier behind the first-line enemy trench, and remained with him all day and night. The next morning he brought the soldier out through the German wire, to rescue him and also two wounded Gurkhas whilst under enemy fire. Rifleman Kulbir Thapa is shown in British 'modified' service dress, with the slouch hat worn with the left side turned up—a style quite common with the Gurkhas at the time. His 'marching order' equipment is the 1903 leather bandolier pattern with haversack, water-bottle, 'smoke helmet' respirator, and blanket rolled

in a groundsheet. His kukri is worn on his right hip beneath the waterbottle, and obscured at the back of his belt is his messtin and entrenching tool. Fastened to his bayonet scabbard at his left side is the entrenching tool handle. His rifle is the .303 inch Short Lee-Enfield Mark III. His only insignia is the title '3G' on his shoulder straps.

In September 1964 Indonesia raided the mainland of Malaya with a force of parachute troops. Of the 96 Indonesian paratroops who dropped, the 1st/10th Gurkhas accounted for no less than 51. Above, kukri in hand, a rifleman of the 1st/10th shepherds a forlorn-looking Indonesian into captivity. The battalion's hat device shows clearly. (Major H. E. Shields)

Figures **D2** and **D3** depict a British captain and a rifleman of the 1st Battalion, 1st Gurkhas in 1915. The officer's uniform is the service dress of a rifle regiment including black buttons, regimental title below the three black stars of his rank on the shoulder straps, and a red cord boss on his cap upon which is the badge of the Regiment—Prince of Wales's coronet and plume with crossed kukris and the numeral 'I'. He carries Sam Browne equipment and a respirator.

The rifleman wears a British-pattern greatcoat over his service dress and a woollen 'cap, comforter'. He displays the rear equipment worn by D1 (less blanket and messtin). Note the carriage of the entrenching tool head and handle, and the canvas cover tied over the scabbard of the kukri. Slung over his right shoulder is a respirator in its haversack. A

In 1974 Gurkhas were flown from the United Kingdom to Cyprus to reinforce the British sovereign base areas on the island. The move caused consternation in the Turkish press, which objected to 'Mercenaries in Her Majesty's uniform'. Above, men of the 10th Gurkhas are seen deplaning in Cyprus. (Major H. E. Shields)

sentry, he peers into a trench periscope, his rifle and bayonet at his side. (Sources: photographs, dress regulations, regimental histories.)

E: The Middle East, 1915–18

In late 1915 the Indian Corps was withdrawn from France, after which the main effort of the Indian Army in the Great War was in the Middle East. The figures on this plate demonstrate the uniform and equipment worn in that theatre at this time.

The central figure, **E3**, depicts a rifleman of the

including black buttons, '10G' shoulder titles, and black good conduct chevrons and skill-at-arms badge. His equipment is still the 1903 bandolier pattern of the previous plate; and he has drawn his kukri to supplement his Short Lee-Enfield rifle and bayonet. The white bands worn on the arms were a field identification sign for the Sari Bair operation.

By 1917 some Gurkha units had been issued with the 1914 pattern leather equipment, the 'fighting order' of which is shown being worn by **E1**, a rifleman of the 2nd/3rd Gurkhas in Palestine, 1917. Note the triangular patches of the 3rd, worn on the hat. Note also the waterbottle worn at the rear of the belt in order to leave access to the kukri.

Figure **E2** shows a lance-naik of the 2nd/5th Gurkhas in Mesopotamia (modern Iraq), 1918. He wears the 1914 pattern leather equipment in 'marching order', which includes pack, steel helmet, respirator, entrenching tool, waterbottle and haversack. Carrying a .303 inch Lewis machine gun, his personal weapons are a pistol and his kukri. Note the green folds on his hat puggaree—a distinction of the 5th Gurkhas. Note also his badge of rank, Lewis Gun skill-at-arms badge, and the four overseas service chevrons. (Sources: photographs, drawings, regimental histories.)

F: Indian Garrisons

The Great War over, the Gurkhas disbanded the war-raised battalions and the 11th Gurkhas and went back to the pre-war duties of garrison life and 'keeping the peace' in India, not the least part of which was maintaining a presence by means of ceremonial. The figures on this plate show typical forms of dress for this type of duty.

Figure **F1** depicts a rifleman of the 1st/8th Gurkhas presenting arms in the 'drill order' of the 1920s. At this time the 1st Battalion wore a red 'plume' in their felt hats similar to the hackle of the Black Watch, commemorating an association with that regiment in the recent war. The plume was worn above a red patch to which was pinned the regimental badge in black metal. The 2nd/8th Gurkhas continued to wear a red 'pompon' above the badge. At about this time the slouch hat—a fairly common item which had been widely worn in the British service—began to develop into the 'Gurkha hat'. This was created by sewing two hats together, one inside the

The 'stone-coloured' No. 6 dress is worn for ceremonial and formal parade purposes in designated 'warm weather' areas. It is worn here by a

Lance-Corporal of the 10th Gurkhas in Hong Kong. Note the regimental badge worn on the Kilmarnock cap and on the belt buckle. (Major H. E. Shields)

2nd Battalion, 10th Gurkhas in the attack at Sari Bair, Gallipoli, in August 1915. Operating with the 1st/5th Gurkhas, New Zealand troops and the 1st/6th Gurkhas, the 10th were part of an effort that might have resulted in a British victory with the capture of Chunuk Bair. The 1st/6th actually reached the vital crest only to be driven off by fire, thought to be from British naval guns (an early example of 'friendly fire'). The rifleman wears the pre-1914 field service hot weather order of a Gurkha regiment. The slouch hat has not yet acquired the style of later years. The khaki drill uniform retains many regimental items

The Gurkha hat as worn in the British Army nowadays. Note the badge of the 10th Gurkhas, worn on a patch of Hunting Stewart tartan; and also the '10GR' shoulder title. (Major H. E. Shields)

other to give a thick, flat brim, with the crease sewn into the crown. A puggaree and a variety of regimental devices were added. The Gurkha hat is always worn with a chinstrap under either the chin or the lower lip, and is usually tilted to the right to some degree. The 8th Gurkhas adopted the practice of wearing strips of coloured cloth on the shoulder straps to indicate each company; pinned to the strips were the shoulder titles. **F1** also wears the medal ribbons of the Great War, three good conduct badges (more than 12 years' service), and the skill-at-arms badge for rifle marksmanship. His equipment is the 1903 Bandolier belt, pouches and frog, and his weapons the Short Lee-Enfield Mk III rifle, bayonet

and kukri. 'Hosetops', footless stockings, and short puttees came into general use for field and drill purposes at this time.

Figure **F3** shows the rear view of drill order, worn by a colour havildar of the 9th Gurkhas in the 1930s. Note the diamond patch worn on the puggaree by the 9th, shoulder titles, badges of rank, and the SMLE carried at the 'shoulder'. Company colours were worn as garter flashes in this regiment.

F2 depicts a piper of the 10th Gurkhas in the late 1930s. The link between the 10th Gurkhas and the Royal Scots is clear from the Hunting Stewart tartan of the pipe bag, fly plaid and lower pipe ribbon and the Royal Stewart upper pipe ribbon. Note the bugle-

Men of the 10th Gurkhas being inspected by a lieutenant (QGO) prior to a parade. Note the No. 6 dress, 5.56mm rifles, and the officer's arm badge. (Major H. E. Shields)

horn incorporated in the cap badge and shoulder belt plate and worn below the shoulder belt buckle. Note also the black buttons and chevrons of a rifle regiment. (The latter indicate lance-naik rank, and good conduct badges for more than five years' service.) Regimental hosetops, garters and spats complete the piper's outfit. (Sources: photographs and regimental histories.)

G: The North-West Frontier, 1930s

The other aspect of the Gurkha regiments' duties in the interwar years was the security of the North-West Frontier of India, an area rarely at peace.

At left, **G1** depicts a havildar of the 2nd/4th Gurkhas in the field service order of 1930 as worn in hot weather. His Gurkha hat has a puggaree with a black upper fold, a regimental distinction, as are the '4G' shoulder title and the black tape badge of rank

worn on the 'greyback' flannel shirt; coloured garter flashes indicate his company. By this time leather equipment had been replaced by webbing, in this case the 1908 pattern infantry set. This is shown with the haversack on the back with the groundsheet strapped below, and with the waterbottle worn below that. The kukri scabbard has a canvas cover; canvas covers were also worn on bayonet scabbards. The havildar's weapon is the Short Lee-Enfield rifle Mk III.

Beside him stands a lance-naik of the 3rd Gurkhas, **G2**. On his puggaree is the triangle patch of the 3rd, and company colours are worn beneath the '3G' shoulder titles. He wears the issue pullover with white badges of rank, and 'chupli' sandals in place of boots and puttees—chuplis were widely worn on the Frontier. His '08 webbing is worn with pack and haversack, and he is armed with a Webley pistol and kukri as personal weapons in addition to the .303 inch Vickers-Berthier light machine gun at his feet. The latter was adopted by the Indian Army in the 1930s as a replacement for the Lewis gun.

In the middle distance **G3**, a naik of the 5th Gurkhas, operates a .303 inch Vickers machine gun, a potent weapon on the Frontier on account of its great range and sustained fire capability. Note the green folds on his hat puggaree, the company colours on his shoulder straps, and the badges of rank on his pullover.

In the distance a signaller of the 4th Gurkhas, **G4**, operates a heliograph. This mirror/lamp equipment was one of the best forms of communication ever devised for the conditions prevailing on the North-West Frontier. Note the numeral 'IV' on the signaller's puggaree.

In the background is the fort at Landi Kotal, one of the outposts which had to be garrisoned if the communications and security of the region were to be maintained. Occupation of the high ground was vital in the wars and skirmishes that flared along the Frontier. 'Picketing'—the rapid seizure, and even more rapid evacuation of vital heights—was a manoeuvre calling for nerve and fitness. Few could picket as well as the Gurkhas. (Sources: photographs and regimental histories.)

Men of the 1st/7th Gurkhas on a FIBUA (fighting in built up areas) range, United Kingdom, 1983. The 1st/7th had only recently returned from the South Atlantic where they took part in the recapture of the Falkland Islands. Note the DPM combat dress, 1958 pattern equipment and the 9mm L2 Sterling sub-machine guns. The black disc sleeve patch is a battalion device; black shaped company patches—triangle, square, etc.—were worn on the right sleeve. (UKLF Bob Fousert)

H: Italy, 1944–45

The outbreak of war in 1939 saw the Gurkha regiments once again committed to action with Indian formations in the Middle East; and it was from this theatre of operations that the war was taken to the Axis when Allied forces landed in Sicily and Italy in 1943. In the hard battles up the length of Italy the Gurkhas found themselves in the mountains, familiar terrain both from their homeland and from their operations on the North-West Frontier of India. Gurkha battalions fought with the three Indian infantry divisions committed to the war in Italy, and also with an independent Gurkha brigade.

Figure **H1** depicts a havildar of the 2nd/6th Gurkhas in the battle order worn during the winter of 1944/45. The 2nd/6th Gurkhas formed part of the 43rd Independent Indian Infantry Brigade, along with the 2nd/8th and 2nd/10th Gurkhas. At the time depicted the Brigade was attached to the British 1st Armoured Division, and wore the rhinoceros sign of that division. The uniform worn by the 2nd/6th havildar is typically Gurkha, with the pullover, battledress trousers and hosetops worn in this way. Note the 1937 pattern webbing equipment, extra bandolier, entrenching tool *and* pick, the battledress blouse rolled in the gas cape atop the haversack, and the kukri in a canvas cover. Note also his badge of rank, and his 'No. 1' rifle and bayonet—as the SMLE had now become. Our subject is a guide for an operation, as evidenced by the torch, tape and tactical sign.

In the bitter winter weather of the Appenines special clothing became available in 1944; the Gurkha rifleman at **H2** is wearing one of the outfits issued for snowy conditions. Worn over normal uniform, it consisted of a white smock and trousers, a white duffle coat, a white helmet cover and mittens. His weapon is a .45 inch Thompson sub-machine gun.

In more temperate climates battledress alone was worn, as shown by **H3**—a British major of the 2nd/3rd Gurkhas, 10th Indian Infantry Division, 1944/45. Note the cap badge of Queen Alexandra's cypher, the black badges of rank, and the wound stripe on the left cuff. In the 10th Indian Division patches were suspended from the shoulder strap on which were sewn the regimental designation (in this case '3 GR'), the divisional sign, and black bars for the brigade—two here for the 20th Indian Infantry Brigade. The Major wears '37 pattern webbing and a .38 inch Enfield No. 2 Pistol. (Sources: photographs, regimental and campaign histories.)

In the background are the ruins of the monastery of Monte Cassino.

I: The Far East, 1941–45

Battalions of the Gurkha regiments made a major contribution in the Far East during the Second World War, both in containing the Japanese invasions and in regaining the territories lost to them.

Figure **I1** shows a naik of the 2nd/9th Gurkhas at the time of the Japanese invasion of Malaya. He wears

The climate of Hong Kong is temperate for part of the year, when No. 2 dress—service dress—is worn. The photograph shows the Adjutant and Regimental Sergeant Major of the 10th Gurkhas in No. 2 dress. Note the Regimental pattern of pouch belts, and the Adjutant's No. 1 dress cap and arm badge. (Major H. E. Shields)

the khaki drill uniform of the time, 1937 pattern webbing equipment, and is armed with a Thompson sub-machine gun. Note his cloth regimental titles, black tape badges of rank, divisional insignia, and company garter flashes. His shorts are the 'Bombay bloomers' designed to be tucked into the hosetops. The 2nd/9th Gurkhas were one of the battalions unfortunate enough to go into Japanese captivity after the fall of Singapore.

By 1945 a much more practical uniform had been adopted, as worn by **I2**, a typical Gurkha rifleman of the period. His denim battledress is of Indian manufacture; equipment is the 1937 pattern webbing; the Gurkha hat was worn with a netting cover to hold camouflage material, and our subject is armed with a .303 inch No. 4 rifle and bayonet in addition to his kukri. The rifle is equipped with a launcher and sights to fire the No. 85 Grenade attached. Spare grenades in their containers are slung behind his back.

The olive green battledress worn by **I3**, also manufactured in India, was much more widely worn and may be considered the standard uniform of 1944–45. **I3** depicts a subedar of 153 (Gurkha) Parachute Battalion in 1945. By this time Indian Army parachute units had adopted the maroon beret of the British airborne troops, worn with a special badge. The parachute qualification 'wings' of the Gurkhas differed from the British pattern, and were sometimes worn on the right breast. Note our subject's badges of rank; and the 1937 pattern webbing set holding a .38 inch Smith and Wesson revolver and ammunition, compass and binoculars. (Sources: photographs and regimental histories.)

In the background can be seen brick pagodas typical of the thousands in and around Mandalay, retaken from the Japanese in March 1945.

J: Far East Garrisons, 1950s–70s

In 1948 units of the British Brigade of Gurkhas were settling into their new homes in Malaya when Communist insurrection flared. This war, which the British chose to call an 'emergency', lasted more than ten years before the Communists were defeated. The Gurkhas made a significant contribution towards the victory, campaigning in some of the worst conditions of climate and terrain against a wily and determined enemy.

The central figure **J2** is a rifleman of the 1st/7th Gurkhas wearing the typical uniform and equipment of the period. Clothing wore out quickly in Malaya, and many patterns from stock were used to clothe the troops on campaign; both British- and Indian-

Piper of the 6th Gurkhas in No. 1 dress: it is plain rifle green throughout, no tartan being worn. Note the pipe banner and the white spats. (Major P. A. Gouldsbury)

manufactured clothing was used up. The only constant was the colour—jungle green. Our subject's equipment is the 1944 pattern webbing, which had been specially designed for jungle warfare. (In the observation of the author, only the Gurkhas wore it as it was intended to be worn.) Even so, the heavy loads carried on operations required much gear to be strapped outside the haversack. The kukri came into its own in Malaya as a jungle knife as well as a weapon—Gurkhas never carried the issue machete. The weapon is the Mk III version of the .303 inch Bren light machine gun; this too had been devised for jungle warfare, and was slightly lighter and shorter than previous versions. Note the white square worn on the jungle hat by the 1st/7th Gurkhas as a recognition sign in 1954. Note also the crossed kukri sign of the 17th Gurkha Division.

Figure **J3** depicts a British officer of the 1st/6th

Gurkhas in 1955. He too wears the jungle green uniform, 'sweat rag', jungle hat and canvas-and-rubber jungle boots similar to J2, but with a different form of webbing. Packs were usually dumped at 'base camps' to facilitate patrolling, leaving the individual with weapon and ammunition, knife, waterbottle and little else; the weapon here is the .30 inch M1 American carbine. Note the 'VI' recognition sign on his jungle hat, and the map and cased compass so vital for jungle navigation.

Out of the jungle the Gurkhas maintained their high standards of turnout and ceremonial. **J1**, a lieutenant (QGO) of the 2nd Gurkhas in the 1970s carries the regimental Truncheon mentioned in the text—a magnificent item featuring a crown supported by Gurkha Riflemen above crossed kukris. Note the dicing and badge on the headdress, the scarlet 'facing' on the collar, the regimental pouch belt, the regimental lanyard, black buttons, and badges of rank and shoulder titles on a strip of ribbon of the Brigade colours. (Sources: photographs and regimental histories.)

K: The 1960s and '70s

Many Gurkhas continue to serve India, represented here by **K1**, a lance-naik of the 5th Gurkhas in the 1960s. The 3rd/1st, 2nd/5th and the 5th/5th served with the Indian Army contingent to the United Nations peace-keeping force in Katanga, former Belgian Congo, dressed and equipped as shown. The green folds in the Gurkha hat puggaree were by now a long-standing tradition, as was the wearing of a scarlet lanyard to commemorate the 5th having been a Royal regiment when in British service. Company colours continued to be worn on the shoulder strap above the shoulder title. Sleeve insignia include a national title, the United Nations' crest and the black tape badge of rank. Equipment and weapon were still the 1937 pattern webbing and the venerable Lee-Enfield No. 1 rifle.

The Kingdom of Nepal maintains an army in which Gurkhas may serve without leaving their homeland; **K2** depicts a junior NCO in one of the Nepalese regiments, the Devi Dutt, in the 1970s.

Rifleman of the 6th Gurkhas on public duties in the United Kingdom. Note the greatcoat worn with No. 2 dress, black gloves and SA 80 rifle. (Major P. A. Gouldsbury)

A fine study of a Gurkha corporal as he prepares to shoot after having traversed an assault course. Note the DPM material with which he has covered the handguard and butt of his rifle. (Major P. A. Gouldsbury)

Note the Kilmarnock cap of the British Gurkhas, worn with a drab serge uniform of an unusual pattern. Badges of rank and equipment are of traditional pattern, and the weapon is the 7.62mm SLR, made in India but of the British L1 design.

Figure **K3** depicts a Gurkha in the British service, in this case Lance-Corporal Rambahadur Limbu, VC, of the 10th Princess Mary's Own Gurkha Rifles. Rambahadur won his Victoria Cross on 21 November 1965 during the Borneo 'Confrontation', when a member of 'C' Company, 2nd/10th Gurkhas. He was in the forefront of his company's attack on a strong Indonesian position, killed the first enemy, and constantly braved enemy fire to carry out his duties as section second-in-command. Above all, for twenty minutes he persisted in supremely brave attempts to save two wounded men and, in spite of intense machine gun fire concentrated on him per-

sonally, he finally succeeded in carrying them to safety. He later rose through the ranks and was awarded a commission; and when this gallant officer finally retired in the late 1980s the British Army lost its last serving holder of the supreme decoration.

Rambahadur is shown in the No. 1 dress of his regiment, wearing the VC he won in Sarawak. His weapon is the L1 self-loading rifle. (Sources: photographs and regimental histories.)

L: The 1980s and '90s

Figure **L1** represents a lieutenant (QGO) of the 6th Gurkhas in the No. 6 dress worn for ceremonial and parade purposes in 'warm weather' areas, 1990s. Note the pouch belt with regimental badge, the pattern of sword carried by officers of rifle regiments, the badges of rank and shoulder titles, and the Prussian Eagle badge of the 14th/20th King's Hussars worn by the 6th Gurkhas as an armbadge to commemorate the association of the regiments in the Second World War.

Figure **L2** depicts the 'drill order' uniform of an

The hat and kukri of a 6th Gurkha. Note the small knife and honing steel, and how much smaller the kukri is when compared with the weapon of 1815. (Major P. A. Gouldsbury)

NCO of the 8th Gurkhas, 1990s. The traditional scarlet 'pompon' is still worn on the Gurkha hat, as is the regimental badge in black metal on a scarlet patch. Company colours continue to be worn on the shoulder straps, beneath titles in the form of the regimental badge. Yet another traditional item of dress is the lanyard. The Indian Army retain green uniforms for 'hot weather' wear, though of a better quality and cut than the olive green of former years. Note the black equipment, and the 7.62mm self-loading rifle.

Far from warm weather was experienced by the 1st/7th Gurkhas in the Falklands War of 1982. Special clothing was needed to combat the extreme cold and wet, and L3 shows a rifleman of the 1st/7th dressed in British Army 'cold weather' (CW) parka, overtrousers and pile cap; many layers of clothing were worn beneath these outer garments. Galoshes and 1958 pattern webbing complete his outfit, and he is armed with the 9mm Sterling L2 sub-machine gun. With combat dress the 1st/7th Gurkhas wore a rifle green beret, cap badge, also black patches in company shapes on the sleeves of the combat smock; but no insignia other than badges of rank were worn on the CW parka. (Sources: photographs and regimental histories.)

BIBLIOGRAPHY

Brigadier E. V. R. Bellers, *The History of the 1st King George V's Own Gurkha Rifles (The Malaun Regiment), Vol. II, 1920–47* (Gale & Polden, Aldershot, 1956).

Harold James and Denis Sheil-Small, *A Pride of Gurkhas—2nd King Edward VII's Own Goorkhas (The Sirmoor Rifles) 1948–1971* (Leo Cooper, London, 1975).

Brigadier C. N. Barclay CBE DSO, *The Regimental History of the 3rd Queen Alexandra's Own Gurkha Rifles, Vol. II, 1927 to 1947* (Wm Clowes & Sons, London, 1953).

Ranald Macdonnell and Marcus Macaulay, *A History of the 4th Prince of Wales's Own Gurkha Rifles 1857–1937, Vols. I and II* (William Blackwood & Sons, Edinburgh and London, 1940).

History of the 5th Royal Gurkha Rifles (Frontier Force), Vol. II, 1919–1947 (Gale & Polden, Aldershot, 1956).

Charles Messenger, *The Steadfast Gurkha— Historical records of the 6th Queen Elizabeth's Own Gurkha Rifles 1948–82* (Leo Cooper, London, 1985).

Col. J. N. Mackay DSO, *History of the 7th Duke of*

Edinburgh's Own Gurkha Rifles (Wm Blackwood, Edinburgh, 1962).

Lt.Col. H. J. Huxford OBE, *History of the 8th Gurkha Rifles* (Gale & Polden, Aldershot, 1952).

Lt.Col. F. S. Poynder MVO OBE MC, *The 9th Gurkha Rifles, Vol. I, 1817–1936* (Butler and Tanner, London, 1937).

10th Gurkha Rifles, One Hundred Years (The Regimental Trust, 10th Princess Mary's Own Gurkha Rifles, Great Britain, 1990).

Maj. G. F. MacMunn, *The Armies of India* (Adam & Charles Black, London, 1911).

Maj. Donovan Jackson, *India's Army* (Sampson Low, Marston & Co., London, 1940).

The Tiger Triumphs (His Majesty's Stationery Office, India, 1946).

Harold James and Denis Sheil-Small, *The Gurkhas* (Macdonald & Co., London, 1965).

Nepal and the Gurkhas (Ministry of Defence, HMSO, London, 1965).

Col. H. C. B. Rogers, *Weapons of the British Soldier* (Sphere Books, London, 1972).

J. B. R. Nicholson, *The Gurkha Rifles*, Osprey MAA41, (Reading, 1974).

Philip Mason, *A Matter of Honour* (Peregrine Books, England, 1976).

Robert Wilkinson-Latham, *North-West Frontier 1837–1947*, Osprey, MAA72, (London, 1977).

Materiel Regulations for the Army, Vol. 3, Clothing (Ministry of Defence, 1980).

Boris Mollo, *The Indian Army* (Blandford Press, Poole, 1981).

Denis Sheil-Small, MC, *Green Shadows: A Gurkha Story* (William Kimber & Co. Ltd, London, 1982).

Byron Farwell, *The Gurkhas* (Allen Lane, Penguin Books, London, 1984).

Christopher Chant, *Gurkha* (Blandford Press, Dorset, 1985).

Lt.Col. J. P. Cross, *In Gurkha Company* (Arms and Armour Press, London, 1986).

Dress Regulations (India) 1931 (Facsimile Print) (Ray Westlake Military Books, Newport, 1987).

Alan Harfield, *The Indian Army of the Empress, 1861–1903* (Spellmount, Tunbridge Wells, 1990).

Army Regulations, India. Volume VII, Dress (Facsimile Print) (Ray Westlake Military Books, Newport, 1991).

John Gaylor, *Sons of John Company* (Spellmount, Tunbridge Wells, 1992).

Eric Neild, *With Pegasus in India* (Jay Birch & Co., Singapore, no date).

Notes sur les planches en couleurs

A1 Un soldat pendant la guerre Anglo-Gurkha de 1814–16, basé sur l'évidence limitée illustrée; à noter le casque porté par dessus un linge sur la tête, et le kukri large porté au devant du corps. **A2** Premier uniforme des Gurkhas connu dans le service anglais, tiré d'une peinture de l'époque; les habits sont en général encore de la région mais on aperçoit cependant le style du régiment anglais Rifle qui s'infiltre. **A3** A partir des années 1820, un uniforme d'un style bien plus européen et formel est disponible.

B1, B3 La Sirmoor Battalion (2nd Gurkhas) se distingue à Delhi en 1857, et certaines peintures et d'anciennes photographies survivent de l'époque. Le bonnet Kilmarnock du soldat anglais est porté sur le haut de la tête, il est empesé et porte le motif en dés du bataillon sur la bande. La couleur et le contour de l'uniforme sont habituels dans le régiment Rifle et on porte le fusil Brunswick. **B2** L'officier porte la tenue pour climat chaud qui est en partie blanche.

C1 Uniforme de combat pour climat chaud en coton couleur khaki, avec une pièce empesée ajoutée à la toque. A noter le numéro du régiment sur les pattes d'épaule – l'unique insigne; équipement ordinaire en cuir de l'Armée de Indes; clairon argenté du régiment Rifle. **C2** Vingt ans plus tard, l'officier britannique porte le short adopté à cette époque; équipement en cuir Sam Browne, casque protège-soleil, sac à dos et mégaphone. **C3** Le casque blanc et l'insigne réglementaire sont les deux seules différences entre la tenue complète de cérémonie de l'officier et la tenue d'une unité Rifle anglaise. **C4** Servant ensemble pendant plusieurs campagnes, les unités Ecossaises et Gurkha forment de bons liens, et certains régiments Gurkha adoptent mêmes des cornemuseurs, portant des uniformes de styles variés, influencés par les écossais. **C5** Officier indigène juste avant que les 1st Gurkhas remplacent leur infanterie légère à manteau rouge par l'uniforme Rifle à manteau vert.

D1 Uniforme de service modifié anglais avec le chapeau mou Gurkha; équipement en cuir Bandolier de 1903, et fusil SMLE. L'unique insigne est le '3G' sur les pattes d'épaule. Tiré d'un portrait de Kulbir Thapa qui obtient la Victoria Cross. **D2** Cet officier porte l'uniforme de service des régiments Rifle avec les boutons et les insignes noirs. **D3** Vue sur l'arrière du même uniforme que chez D1, sauf qu'il comprend le manteau et la casquette en tricot.

Farbtafeln

A1 Soldat im Anglo-Gurkha-Krieg 1814–16 gemäß spärlichen Bildmaterials; man beachte den Helm, der über einem Kopftuch getragen wird, und den großen Kukri am Oberkörper. **A2** Erste bekannte Uniform der Gurkhas im britischen Dienst, einem zeitgenössischen Gemälde nachempfunden; die Kleidung ist größtenteils noch einheimisch, spiegelt jedoch bereits den Stil des britischen Rifle-Regiments. **A3** In den 20er Jahren des 19. Jahrhunderts waren Uniformen vorhanden, die viel europäischer und formeller waren.

B1, B3 Das Sirmoor Battalion (2nd Gurkhas) zeichnete sich 1857 in Delhi aus. Gemälde und frühe Fotografien sind erhalten. Der Kilmarnock-Hut des britischen Soldaten saß hoch auf dem Kopf, war versteift und hatte gewürfelte Battalions-zeichen am Hutband. Die Farbe und der Schnitt der Uniform war jetzt für ein Rifle-Regiment zur Regel geworden, und man trug das Brunswick-Gewehr. **B2** Der Offizier trägt teilweise weiß, die Kleidung für warmes Wetter.

C1 Felduniform für warmes Wetter aus khakifarbener Baumwolle mit versteiftem Nackenschutz an der 'Pillbox'-Mütze. Man beachte die Regimentsnummer auf den Schulterklappen, das einzige Abzeichen; Standardlederausrüstung der indischen Armee und silberfarbenes Signalhorn eines Rifle-Regiments. **C2** Zwanzig Jahre später trägt ein britischer Offizier die kurzen Hosen, die etwa um diese Zeit angenommen wurden; Sam Browne-Lederausrüstung; Tropenhelm, Rucksack und Megaphon. **C3** Offiziersuniform, die sich von der einer britischen Rifle-Einheit lediglich durch den weißen Helm und das Regimentsabzeichen unterscheidet. **C4** Die schottischen Einheiten und die Gurkhas waren bei vielen Feldzügen gemeinsam im Einsatz und gingen eine enge Verbindung ein. Einige Gurkha-Regimente schafften sich Dudelsackpfeifer mit verschiedenen halb-schottischen Uniformen an. **C5** Einheimischer Offizier der Zeit, kurz bevor die 1. Gurkhas von der Uniform der leichten Infanterie mit roter Jacke zur Rifle-Uniform mit grüner Jacke überwechselten.

D1 Abgeänderte britische Militäruniform mit dem Schlapphut der Gurkhas, Bandolier-Lederausrüstung aus dem Jahr 1903 und dem SMLE-Gewehr. Das einzige Abzeichen ist das '3G' auf den Schulterklappen. Einem Porträt von Kulbir Thapa nachempfunden, der mit dem Victoria Cross ausgezeichnet wurde. **D2** Der

E1 Uniforme de combat khaki d'avant 1914 avec l'équipement en cuir de 1914; à noter que les 3rd Gurkhas portent un insigne triangulaire sur le chapeau. E2 Feuille de route complète avec le grand sac, le casque et respirateur, et la mitrailleuse légère Lewis, etc. L'insigne 'd'habileté' est porté au dessus du chevron de rang. Les plis verts dans le puggaree du chapeau identifie les 5th Gurkhas. E3 Les brassards blancs sont des signes d'identification temporaires portés lors d'une attaque à Sari Bair, Gallipoli, en Août 1915; il porte l'équipement Bandolier de 1903.

F1 Le pompon rouge du chapeau est caractéristique au 1st Battalion, 8th Gurkhas; à noter l'insigne au dessous. Le chapeau mou devient maintenant de plus en plus formel, les Gurkhas portent souvent deux chapeaux cousus l'un à l'autre pour les rendre plus raides et élégants. Les pattes de couleur aux épaules identifient les compagnies à l'intérieur des bataillons. F2 Les cornemuseurs des 10th Gurkhas portent des articles en tissu écossais qui rappellent leur association avec les Royal Scots. F3 L'insigne sur le chapeau est caractéristique chez les 9th Gurkhas qui attachent des rubans du coloris de leur compagnie à leurs guêtres. Ce sous-officier supérieur montre l'arrière du même uniforme qu'en F1.

G1 Insigne régimental sur les pattes d'épaule et au puggaree; chemise grise ordinaire et le short couleur khaki, équipement d'ordonnance de 1908 appartenant à l'uniforme de l'Armée Britannique pour climat chaud. G2 Ce membre de l'équipe de mitrailleurs Vickers-Berthier porte l'équipement de pistolet. A la Frontière, on porte souvent les tricots et des sandales chupli au lieu de bottes. G3, G4 Mitrailleur moyen Vickers, signaleur d'héliographe qui porte les distinctions des 5th et 4th Gurkhas au chapeau.

H1 Havildar (sergent) de la 2nd Bn., 6th Gurkhas en Italie, pendant l'hiver de 1944. En service dans la British 1st Armoured Division, il en porte l'insigne bouclée par dessus ses pattes d'épaule, qui sont elles-mêmes passées à travers des fentes dans son tricot. H2 Habits spéciaux distribués pour très mauvais temps. H3 Le chef britannique du 2nd Bn., 3rd Gurkhas, 10th Indian Division démontre les pratiques des insignes à l'intérieur de cette division: rabat à l'épaule qui pend portant les titres régimentaux, le signe de la division et deux barres noires qui indiquent la deuxième brigade de la division.

I1 Naik (caporal), Malaisie en 1942, porte essentiellement le même uniforme que celui porté pendant les années 1930 sur la Frontière Nord-Ouest, bien qu'on le voit maintenant avec l'équipement d'ordonnance de 1937 et le fusil Thompson. I2 Uniforme de combat vert, léger et plus pratique, porté pendant les dernières campagnes en Birmanie; on distribue des casques mais on porte plus souvent le chapeau lors du combat, tel qu'on le voit ici avec le voile de camouflage. Son fusil no.4 a une grenade no.85 attachée à la bouche. I3 Béret de parachutiste et brevet à la manche; équipement d'ordonnance de l'officier de 1937. A noter les insignes aux pattes d'épaule de l'officier indigène.

J1 Officier des 2nd Gurkhas portant l'uniforme de cérémonie tropical avec les distinctions complètes du régiment, portant le Truncheon qui remplace les drapeaux dans cette unité. J2 Mitrailleur Bren habillé de la tenue typique de la campagne en Malaisie des années 1950; à noter l'insigne sur le chapeau de la 1st Bn., 7th Gurkhas et l'insigne à la manche de la 17th Gurkha Division; équipement d'ordonnance à motif de 1944. J3 A noter l'insigne régimentale des 6th Gurkhas sur le chapeau, l'équipement léger porté pendant les patrouilles de courte distance et la carabine US M1.

K1 Pendant le service aux Indes, et faisant partie ici des forces de l'UN à Katanga au Zaïre, il porte le chapeau du régiment, les distinctions aux pattes d'épaule, et, en dessous, le titre national 'India' à la manche et l'insigne de l'UN. K2 L'uniforme d'un sous-officier Gurkha junior du régiment Devi Dutt de la Royal Nepalese Army. K3 Uniforme de cérémonie no.1 des 10th Gurkhas de l'Armée Britannique, peint à partir de photographies du Lance-Corporal Rambahadur Limbu qui obtient la Victoria Cross à Sarawak en 1965.

L1 Tenue de cérémonie pour climat chaud porté par un officier britannique. Les 6th Gurkhas portent l'Aigle Prussienne des 14th/20th Hussars à la manche car il forment de bons liens ensemble pendant la Deuxième Guerre Mondiale. L2 Sous-officier des 8th Gurkhas, Armée des Indes; le pompon rouge est maintenant plus grand; on porte l'insigne du régiment aux pattes d'épaule sur une bandelette du coloris de la compagnie. L3 Parka d'hiver de l'Armée Britannique, sur-pantalons et casquette d'hiver, équipement d'ordonnance de 1958 porté par un soldat de la 1st Bn., 7th Gurkhas pendant la campagne des Falklands en 1982.

Offizier trägt den Dienstanzug des Rifle-Regiments mit schwarzen Knöpfen und Abzeichen. D3 Rückansicht des praktisch gleichen Anzugs wie auf D1, doch hier mit Überzieher und Strickmütze.

E1 Khaki-Felduniform vor 1914 mit 1914er Lederausrüstung; man beachte das Dreiecksabzeichen der 3rd Gurkhas auf dem Hut. E2 Volle Marschausrüstung mit großem Tornister, Helm, Umhängegasmaske etc. und leichtes Lewis-Maschinengewehr – das entsprechende Waffentauglichkeitsabzeichen wird über dem Rangwinkel getragen. Grüner Streifen im Hutband kennzeichnen die 5th Gurkhas. E3 Bei den weißen Armbinden handelt es sich um zeitweilige Erkennungszeichen, die für einen Angriff in Sari Bair, Gallipoli, im August 1915 getragen wurden; er trägt 1903er Bandolier-Ausrüstung.

F1 Die rote Hutquaste machte das 1st Battalion, 8th Gurkhas erkenntlich; man beachte das Abzeichen darunter. Der Schlapphut wurde nun formeller; die Gurkhas trugen zwei ineinander genähte Hüte, die so steifer und ordentlicher aussahen. Farbige Streigen an den Schulterklappen kennzeichneten einzelne Kompanien innerhalb eines Bataillons. F2 Pfeifer der 10th Gurkhas trugen Schottenmuster, die an ihre Verbindung mit The Royal Scots erinnerten. F3 Das Abzeichen am Hut war ein Kennzeichen der 9th Gurkhas, die am Strumpfband ihrer Socken Bänder in den Farben der Kompanie trugen. Dieser dienstältere Unteroffizier zeigt die Rückseite der gleichen Uniformordnung wie auf F1.

G1 Regimentsabzeichen an der Schulterklappe und Hutband; Standardhemd in grau und khakifarbene kurze Hosen, 1908er Gurtausrüstung des Feldanzugs der britischen Armee für heiße Wetterbedingungen. G2 Dieser Schütze einer Vickers-Berthier-Maschinengewehrmannschaft trägt Pistolenausrüstung. Pullover und Chupli-Sandalen anstelle von Stiefeln waren an der Nordwest-Grenze geläufig. G3, G4 Vickers-Maschinengewehr-Schütze und Heliographmelder zeigen Regimentsabzeichen der 5th und 4th Gurkhas an der Mütze.

H1 Havildar (Unteroffizier) der 2nd Bn., 6th Gurkhas, im Winter 1944 in Italien. Er dient im britischen 1st Armoured Division und trägt das entsprechenden Abzeichen über die Schulterklappen, die durch Schlitze im Pullover gezogen sind, geschlungen. H2 Sonderkleidung, die für sehr kalte Wetterbedingungen ausgegeben wurde. H3 Britischer Major des 2nd. Bn., 3rd Gurkhas, 10th Indian Division demonstriert, wie in dieser Division Abzeichen getragen wurden: eine hängende Schulterklappe mit Regimentsbezeichnung, Divisionszeichen und zwei schwarze Streifen, die die zweite Brigade innerhalb der Division bezeichneten.

I1 Naik (Obergefreiter), Malaiischer Bund 1942, in praktisch der gleichen Uniform, wie sie in den 30er Jahren an der Nordwest-Grenze getragen wurde, doch jetzt mit 1937er Gurtausrüstung und einem Thompson-Gewehr. I2 Der praktische, leichte grüne Kampfanzug, der in späteren Birma-Feldzügen getragen wurde; zwar wurden Helme ausgegeben, doch wurde im Gefecht oft die Mütze getragen, hier mit Tarnungsnetz. An der Mündung seines Nr. 4-Gewehres ist eine Nr. 85-Granate befestigt. I3 Fallschirmjäger-Barett und Ärmelbrevet; 1937er Offiziersgurtausrüstung. Man beachte die Schulterklappenabzeichen des einheimischen Offiziers.

J1 Offizier der 2nd Gurkhas in Paradetropenuniform mit allen Regimentsabzeichen und dem Truncheon, der in dieser Einheit die Standarte ersetzte. J2 Bren-Schütze in der typisch malaiischen Felduniform der 50er Jahre; man beachte das Mützenabzeichen des 1st Bn., 7th Gurkhas sowie das Ärmelabzeichen der 17th Gurkha Division; Gurtausrüstung nach 1944er Muster. J3 Man beachte das Regimentshutabzeichen der 6th Gurkhas, wenige Gurte für die Kurzsteckenpatrouille und US M1-Karabiner.

K1 Er dient im indischen Militär und trägt hier, als Teil der UN-Streitmacht in Katanga in Zaire, den Regimentshut, Abzugsleine auf den Schulterklappen, den Landestitel 'India' am Ärmel und das UN-Abzeichen darunter. K2 Die Uniform eines jungen Gurkha-Unteroffiziers im Devi Dutt-Regiment, Königliche Nepalesische Armee. K3 Paradeuniform Nr. 1 der 10th Gurkhas, Britische Armee, als Vorlage für das Gemälde dienten Fotografien von Lance-Corporal Rambahadur Limbu, der 1965 in Sarawak mit dem Victoria Cross ausgezeichnet wurde.

L1 Paradeuniform für heißes Wetter eines Offiziers im britischen Militär. Die 6th Gurkhas tragen den Preussischen Adler der 14th/20th Hussars als Ärmelabzeichen, zu denen sie im Zweiten Weltkrieg enge Verbindung hatten. L2 Unteroffizier, 8th Gurkhas, Indische Armee; der Hut mit der roten Quaste ist inzwischen größer geworden; das Regimentsabzeichen wird auf Schlaufen in den Farben der Kompanie an den Schulterklappen getragen. L2 Parka und Überhosen für kaltes Wetter der britischen Armee, Wintermütze, 1958er Gurtausrüstung an einem Soldat des 1st Bn., 7th Gurkhas 1982 auf den Falkland Inseln.